D1501388

# "Okay, Girls - Man Your Bunks!"

## by Helen Gilbert

Pedestrian Press

Toledo, Ohio

ISBN # 0-9626506-0-9
Printed in the United States of America
Design by Jeff Nelson

Second Printing

For information or to order additional books, please contact:

Pedestrian Press
Post Office Box 4633
Toledo, Ohio 43610-0633

www.PedestrianPress.com

# WAVES

Women Accepted for Volunteer Emergency Service

# Acknowledgements

First, I want to thank my friend Jeff Nelson; your interest in my experiences as a WAVE during World War II inspired me to start writing it all down. You stood by me over the years, and encouraged me to expand the story to encompass my entire life. In addition, your help with the graphics, editing, and production were invaluable. This is as much your book as it is mine. My heartfelt thanks to you.

RoseMarie Bolla was also there for me with encouragement and support along the way.

*Foreword*

*At this point in time I am an 86-year-old great-grandmother, a widow, and living quite an active life. Looking back on my years on this planet, I realize daily how fortunate I have been. To tell the truth, I'm surprised every morning that I am still here and able to get out of my bed. Once that has been established, I retrieve the morning paper from the driveway, get the good old coffee pot brewing, then settle in for an hour or so. Next come the crossword puzzles, morning news from Matt and Katie, my quota of cigarettes, and starting the day with gratitude. I'm sure nicotine and caffeine are the two drugs that keep me going, much to the chagrin of my doctors (it takes a fleet of them to keep me alive).*

*When I first started writing of my experiences during World War II, I had to cast my mind back some sixty years, and recall things I'd done while in my early twenties. The mind is a funny thing, and recalling one thing invariably jarred loose an often unrelated memory. I suddenly remembered people I hadn't thought about in years (some names have been changed to protect their privacy). One thing led to another, and I ended up with a tale of my whole life. The process of piecing it all together led me to reexamine many parts of my life, and it has helped me put it all in perspective.*

*As the scope of the book grew and I delved into my experiences during the Depression, I came to realize that the hardships we endured and the ingenuity generated during those lean years no doubt prepared our generation for facing World War II, with all its consequences.*

*This saga I've written on my computer (which has a life of its own) is how I recall things happening. Naturally I've had my ups and downs - who hasn't? I have many wonderful memories, along with some not so wonderful ones. For me, the bottom line is that I've survived. Being surrounded by loving, caring, somewhat dysfunctional and maybe slightly crazy family and friends no doubt spiced up my time on this planet. I hope I've added some spice to theirs as well.*

*So, without further delay -*

*Here's Helen ....*

# Contents

# Part I

# Early Childhood

## Five to a Bed

My entrance into this world was not glamorous. I was born December 20, 1919. My father was James Lackey Edgar, and my mother was Emma Edgar, nee Harm. I was their second child. My brother James had been born November 24, 1916. At this point in time we lived on Bailey Street, in what I believe it is now considered downtown Philadelphia. Evidently when Mom was in labor with me, she went to use the bathroom, and I popped out on the tile floor. That just might have something to do with my relationship with bathrooms. I keep track of their location at all times in case I need one, and the older I get, the more I seem to need them.

During my early years my mother, father, brother Jim and I had other relatives living with us at times. Mother's brother John and his wife Mae and their two children, Betty and Frank, were with us for a while. After the death of Mom's mother, her stepfather and two stepsisters, Ruth and Hazel, also lived with us. As I begin this chronicle please keep in mind that if any of the relationships and the people in my life I try to tell you about confuse you, think how we must have felt being raised in the midst of them.

—          —          —

I was the youngest of the kids in our family. My brother Jim was three years older, and my Aunt Ruth (Mother's stepsister) was about the same age as Jim. My cousin Betty was also a few years my senior. That meant they had to take care of me, and they didn't like it a bit.

What comes to mind is sleeping in a crowded double bed with my brother Jim, Aunt Ruth, and my cousin Betty. This practice came from Ireland, where they put all the kids in one bed, alternating heads and feet. I was a bed-wetter back then and got into a lot of trouble with my companions when I would have an "accident." It meant changing sheets and created chaos during the night. They were not happy campers.

They were always playing tricks on me, like salting my ice cream when I wasn't looking, or daring me to climb around a steep hillside by the railroad tracks at Penn Station. I fell down and scraped my knees during one of those escapades and they really caught it from my grandmother.

One day my Aunt Mae came by and caught them hanging me out of the third story window of our house by my ankles, getting me to reach down as far as I could. Poor Aunt Mae said she didn't know what to do – if she screamed or snuck up on them they might get startled and drop me. She quietly and calmly came upstairs and told them gently to bring me back in.

Another crisis averted. They were older and I just seemed to do whatever they demanded of me. I was such a nerd! It never occurred to me that I could just say *"I'll tell Mom or Grandmom"* and they would stop.

–        –        –

I was named after my grandmother Helen. She had a face sort of like a Cabbage Patch Doll, with a large nose, pudgy flesh, and twinkling, loving eyes. Her hair was streaked with grey, worn on top of her head in a bun. She was short and fat. It was wonderful to snuggle in her lap and melt into that expanse of softness. She always wore a blue-and-white striped apron over her house dress and smelled of Fels Naphtha, a strong clean laundry soap. Some of our biggest sibling fights were over whose turn it was to visit Grandmom. Jim and I took turns going to her house for the weekend, where we were completely spoiled. I think my mother was jealous of how much we loved our Grandmom, but on the other hand was glad when we were gone for the weekend and she had some time to herself.

For the most part, our living rooms were not used. You were only allowed to open the closed doors briefly, to look. They were for special company, for show, or for funerals. This always puzzled me. It was a treat when favorite Aunts and Uncles would visit, and we actually got to use those rooms.

I grew to hate them, however, after my grandmother Helen died and was laid out in our living room. I was five years old, and to this day remember coming down the stairs of our house and seeing the doors open to our living room, my loving Grandmom in a coffin, on ice. God, what a sadistic ritual. She died at a relatively early age, due to cancer that I heard they thought was from taking diet pills. That was about 1925, so I doubt they really knew.

She passed away on Mother's Day, and I lost the one person who babied and cuddled me. She was my safe haven and always protected me. We kids had chipped in our allowances and bought flowers for her on Mother's Day, but when she died, we reluctantly gave them to Mother instead. It was the one thing our family could laugh about at such a sad time.

This was my first time dealing with the death of a loved one, and I felt abandoned and terrified. I can still recall wondering where she had gone and whether she would be all right. During the evening of the "viewing," all the men were packed in the kitchen, drinking, talking, and smoking, while the women gathered in the dining room and living room, grieving and crying. It was a typical Irish wake. We children went out front to sit on the steps. We were trying to figure out what death was all about. I remember looking up at the night sky and trying to find her in the stars. If she had gone to Heaven, perhaps I could see her.

The funeral itself was a nightmare. My brother Jim actually tried to jump into the grave after the coffin was lowered, to just be with her. There was a lot of wailing and moaning and all I recall is chaos and grief. I have no memory of being consoled by my mother. I was more or less ignored. The whole family was occupied with themselves and their own personal grief. Maybe when we lose a loved one, it is too painful to think of others.

—     —     —

The first house I remember was a three-story brick row-house on 19th Street in Philadelphi, where we lived in the 1920s. They were cheaper to build than single, detached homes, and their shared walls made them easier to heat. They had white limestone steps leading to the front door. We called them "stoops," and they also served as our front porch.

One of my earliest memories is having to go out in the back yard to our toilet, an outhouse. We grew honeysuckle around it in the summer, which smelled good, but in no way did it kill the stink. Going out in the winter was torture, but when you have to go, you have to go! We had chamber pots under our beds for nighttime use. My brother Jim was a sleepwalker when he was younger. One night he got up and urinated in Dad's shoe in the closet in his sleep. We didn't even try to figure out how that happened.

As I recall, our bathtub was a huge wooden vat, in Grandmom's kitchen. We went there on Saturday night and got scrubbed. They put us in one by one and, being the youngest, naturally I was last. That meant being dunked in water left by the others.

At that time we had a Model T Ford, lovingly called the "Tin Lizzie." It was an open touring car, with no windows. Trips in the back seat of that car in the winter involved being wrapped in blankets and still freezing.

We did not have radio but did have an old RCA Victrola with a big horn for sound. Grandmom's favorite song was *"Silver Threads among the Gold."* Oh, those days seem so basic and simple.

We invented our own entertainment in those days. Later, when we were lucky enough to get a nickel and telephones became more common, we would go across the street to the drug store, squeeze into the booth and call a man named Charley. His number was Allegheny 1234. We just dialed that number randomly one day. He must have been retired and lonely, for he would talk to us for as long as we hung on. Can you imagine how stimulating those conversations must have been?

Our playground was the street. The only traffic was a few horse-and-wagons, and later, an automobile or two. We played red light, hop scotch, jump rope, marbles and hide-and-go-seek. Hurdy-gurdies (small merry-go-rounds) came by on a wagon drawn by a horse. It was a miniature contraption with canned music, and a ride cost a penny or two. We loved it.

Rag men sang, *"Any old rags?"* to entice housekeepers to bring out their old rags, which would be recycled. Horseradish men with a large grinder on the wagon showed up every week or so, selling freshly ground horseradishes. Newspapers were sold on the street by boys, and I can still hear them shouting, *"EXTRA, EXTRA, Read all about It !"* We had a lot of action with all the vendors. On the corners where we lived we had a meat market, a drug store, and a bakery .

Our baked goods were beyond description, especially a crisp butter-topped custard coffee cake we ate frequently. A mystery to me is how they made it. The aroma of our small markets sharpened the appetite.

Any small change we got was usually from Grandmom, for candy. I had the idea she was really wealthy, giving away nickels to all of us. We could buy a lot of candy for a penny, so a nickel was a fortune! Standing in the store in front of a glass front counter was a glorious experience, trying to make the best choice. One favorite of mine were the strips of paper lined with little round sugar candies that you had to pick or nibble off.

—　　—　　—

Dad would walk me to an ice cream parlor a few blocks away on summer evenings. We would take a fluted bowl, decorated with gold filigree and hand painted roses. For a quarter we could purchase 6 large scoops of ice cream. It was Breyers ice cream and Dad's favorite flavor was vanilla. These were precious moments for me; to have my Dad to myself was a treat.

Dad had his own business in the early '20s, wiring houses for electricity. Later the business failed. His employees were dishonest and robbed him blind. He was such a trusting soul.

—　　—　　—

At school our classrooms had wooden desks and chairs with cast-iron bases bolted to the floor, and a big blackboard across the front of the room behind the teacher's desk. We hung our coats and put our overshoes in a long narrow closet in the class room. When the weather was cold, rainy or snowy, the boys wore corduroy pants. Let me tell you, damp corduroy pants on unwashed bodies reek. A bath a week was normal then, so none of us smelled that good to begin with. Musty is the word that comes to mind.

Indoor plumbing and electricity were just beginning to be installed in our homes. In the second grade, I was the teacher's pet. The teacher's name was Miss Manning. She reminded me of my grandmother, short and somewhat chubby. She wore all black and was one of the unusual teachers we come across during our school years. She cared enough to make me feel special.

Discipline was not questioned - a good slap on the hand by a ruler was normal. If the behavior was too bad, we were sent to the coat closet or principal's office.

It's sad, but in this day and age of computers, cell phones and other electronic gadgets, it seems like basic skills aren't stressed as much as I think they should be. Education was more straightforward back then; learning to read, write and do arithmetic was our main focus. Spelling was drilled into us at all times, and we had many spelling bees. Penmanship was of the utmost im-portance, and we practiced cursive writing over and over. Mom spent hours with me, helping me learn my multiplication tables while she was ironing. It is the one memory I have of being that close to her.

## Don't Look Up My Family Tree !

My mother was born in the late 1800's to a John Harm and Nellie Murphy. The mixture was Dutch and Irish as far as I know. She had an older brother named John. Her father was into local politics, and was a brick layer. He evidently did quite well financially. He was killed in an accident while working on a reservoir in North Philadelphia. He suffered a broken back and succumbed on the way to the hospital, riding in a horse drawn wagon. The ride would have been down Broad Street, bouncing him over cobblestones all the way to the hospital. His death was evidently traumatic for Mom and I do not believe she ever got over it. Mother was about 10 years old when he died, and her brother John was 13. She was her Dad's pet and she adored him. Over the years, we heard a lot about what a wonderful man he was.

Mom's mother remarried years later to a man named Billie Evans. He was a small man, painfully thin, had lung problems, smoked cigarettes and coughed constantly. Billie kept to himself, in his bedroom, no doubt to stay clear of Mother, who resented him and showed it. The final blow was when they had two girls, Hazel and Ruth. Ruth was born around the same time as my brother Jim. This was a total embarrassment to Mother. To have a child born around the same time as her mother gave birth was more than she could handle.

Uncle John, Mom's brother, was called "Horseshit Johnny" as a child, due to the fact he hung around the stables with the horses. He was a man's man, and liked to gamble. He had coal black hair, olive skin, a large nose and seductive smile. He was rough but gentle, and a smart business man. His theory on travel was why bother? All trees were the same, no matter where they grew. He couldn't understand why I would travel across the country each time I had a new baby – they all looked alike to him.

I made my own Christmas cards in the early '50s and I heard he told my mother, *"For Pete's sake, tell her to try Hallmark. They do a much better job."*

He had married young, to a Catholic girl named Rose. They had a son but divorced when the baby was quite young. I heard that Rose told the boy that his father was dead and would not allow Uncle John to see him. They lost contact with each other over the years.

Later he married Aunt Mae, who had two children from a previous marriage, Betty and Francis. That made them our "shirt tail" cousins. John and Mae eventually had two boys named Billy and Eddie. They were always regarded as "real" cousins. Are you still with me?

When I left to join the Navy in 1942, Uncle John told me if I ever needed anything, to call and he would help. Until the day he died, I knew he meant it and was there for me. I adored him. There was nothing about him that was not real and down to earth. When he was terminal with cancer in 1969, I felt it was important to go to him and share how having him in my life had given me such security. When I arrived the first thing out of his mouth was, *"Well, kid, I suppose you came back to say goodbye?"* My response was, *"I sure did!"* Our heart-to-heart talk eased the pain of losing him.

− − −

My memories of Christmas are bizarre. The adults would put all the kids to bed on Christmas Eve. This would be Jimmy, Ruth, Betty and me. They would then proceed to put up a huge platform in the living room. The Christmas tree would be put in the left back corner. We had a set of Lionel trains and a village scene that was set up on the platform, with the train tracks around the perimeter. There was a train depot, little houses with tree lights inside, and mountains were formed around the base of the decorated tree with some sort of green and brown heavy paper. It was magical to be awakened around 4 am. and come down the stairs to that sight, of course believing that Santa himself had done it.

After Grandmom's death in 1925, it was tradition for us to go to Rosewood Cemetery to her grave on Christmas Day. This was done by caravan. Uncle John, Aunt Mae, Betty and Hazel and Ruth would be in their car. We would be in our Model T. Somehow or other the routine always ended with a family dispute. Lots of angry words and tears. It probably had a lot to do with the grief and love for Grandmom. They simply did not have a clue as to how to deal with those emotions.

Following that depressing trip, we would return to Uncle John's house for dinner. They were no longer living with us. Aunt Mae would take an overdone rump roast out of the oven, open up a can of string beans or peas, and that was our Christmas.

—     —     —

Aunt Mae was a favorite of mine. She would hold me on her lap  and sing sad songs. After much research I found the words to the one I liked best; it could always get me crying and Aunt Mae would comfort me.

*"Little Boy Blue"* by Eugene Field

*The little toy dog is covered with dust,*
*But sturdy and staunch he stands;*
*And the little toy soldier is red with rust,*
*And his musket molds in his hands.*
*Time was when the little toy dog was new,*
*And the soldier was passing fair;*
*And that was the time when our Little Boy Blue*
*Kissed them and put them there.*

*"Now, don't you go till I come," he said,*
*"And don't you make any noise!"*
*So, toddling off to his trundle-bed,*
*He dreamt of the pretty toys;*
*And, as he was dreaming, an angel song*
*Awakened our Little Boy Blue –*
*Oh! The years are many, the years are long,*
*But the little toy friends are true!*
*Aye, faithful to Little Boy Blue they stand,*
*Each in the same old place –*
*Awaiting the touch of a little hand,*
*The smile of a little face;*

My Father in the Navy in WWI.          My parents during the Depression.

L to R: family friend Merle Ritting, Aunt Ruth, Helen, Aunt Hazel, & Jim at the beach.

# "Okay, Girls, Man Your Bunks!"

*And they wonder, as waiting the long years through*
*In the dust of that little chair,*
*What has become of our Little Boy Blue,*
*Since he kissed them and put them there.*

What I know for sure is that I liked being with Aunt Mae and how she made me feel - loved and special. She had bleached blond hair, pale blue eyes and white skin. She was definitely not elegant or classy but solid and earthy. Her house was so full of knickknacks there was not an empty spot on any surface. She loved the five-and-ten-cent stores.

Betty was about the same age as Jim and Ruth, and she and I were pretty close. We made scrapbooks of old movie stars together. She was always more willing than Jim or Ruth to take care of me and do the baby sitting. Her personality was a lot like that of her mother. She was an attractive, blue-eyed blond with a great figure. Her personality was outgoing and she was always fun to be with.

The two boys, Billy and Eddie, were younger. They had their own activities and did not hang out with us very much.

Ruth was my brother's age. She had olive skin, full lips, brown hair and a medium build. She was a quiet, serious soul with a dry sense of humor. The only thing she would order in a restaurant was a grilled cheese sandwich, believing it was safe, that there was not much they could do to spoil it. One thing she did was allow me to tag along on activities like sledding or skating. That made me feel grown up.

She ended up marrying Aunt Mae's brother, and they took off and moved to Oklahoma City. They probably wanted to put as much distance between themselves and the family as possible.

We all gave up trying to figure out how their marriage changed the exact description of our relationships with each other. It was just too complicated.

—    —    —

Hazel was a slim brunette with a small nose, thin lips, and a good build. Just old enough for me to idolize her and think she was the living end. She went on dates, wore makeup and worked. How I wanted to be just like her! This was, of course, the flapper age and she was the typical flapper.

Later I found that she had an affair for years with a married man named Leonard. During a breakup with him, she met and married Bob Culbertson, who was a conductor on a trolley car. Well, that didn't last – apparently Bob went out one night for a pack of cigarettes and never came back. Leonard's

10

name was mentioned in that drama. Uncle John always said that Hazel's problem was that one man was never enough. I do know that Aunt Hazel cried and fainted a lot during the next several years.

–      –      –

Mother had a friend, Ann Roscoe, whose parents lived in Woodbury, New Jersey. They were country folk and lived in a wooden house adjacent to a railroad track. They would take care of us kids for weekends while our parents went on trips to the New Jersey seashore, usually Wildwood.

We called them Mom Mom and Pop Pop. Their house had a stale rancid odor. Pop Pop smoked a pipe. His tobacco and juice would drip down his front, permanently staining his striped shirt and wool vest. He couldn't move around much and spent most of his time in a big chair. Mom Mom had facial hair, bordering on a moustache, and she always wore the same house dress covered with a dirty apron. They were both overweight and they seemed ancient to us. We really enjoyed being out of the city. It was not what I would call a clean environment, but it was full of love. They allowed us complete freedom to play in their yard, walk along the railroad tracks and go wherever we wanted.

One frequent choice was an old cemetery nearby. We would spend hours there, playing among the headstones, reading them to find out who all was buried there. We also played on the railroad tracks. Jim and Ruth would warn me about the third rail. If I accidentally stepped on it, I would die on the spot. To this day I do not know if it was true, but they sure could scare me.

–      –      –

These were the individuals I remember from my early years. Our household had a real mix of people, but they were all considered family. There were lots of skeletons in our closets, things the adults kept from us but whispered about. Therapy was not even heard of, much less considered, so all of the anger, resentment, fear, and guilt were buried within. Emotions ran rampant. Life went on, looking normal until someone or something would trigger an eruption. Then all hell would break loose.

Most of the time we kids just did our thing; when things got out of hand, we would be sent upstairs or outside. Today our family would be labeled "dysfunctional," and were we ever!

I have not mentioned my Dad's family. We did not see too much of them during my early childhood. My Dad's mother had raised seven children, worked hard all her life and was not too enthused about grandchildren. They had four boys and three girls and in those days it was not uncommon to lose a few babies at birth or an early age.

It was rumored they had to eat in shifts, as they had more kids than chairs. When they came to this country from Ireland because of the potato famine, she worked for wealthy folks who lived in the area of Philadelphia called the Main Line. Sunday dinner at her house was a real treat. She was a gourmet cook, and the food was prepared to perfection. I would go to her house occasionally and would feel tolerated, at best. I do remember sitting in her kitchen watching her beat the batter for an orange chiffon cake by hand with a wooden spoon. It seemed to me she kept beating for hours.

I was impressed by her agility and fortitude. Looking back, she was a beautiful woman. She had white hair worn in a bun on top of her head, fine, even features, and clear blue eyes.

Dad's father was a mystery. He was "black Irish" with coal black hair and moustache and heavy black eyebrows. I heard vague stories about him being cruel to the children when they were little. One story was that at Christmas he would put coal in their stockings and tell them it was because they were bad kids. I do believe he was an alcoholic, but in those days it was not recognized or treated as an illness, just something to be hidden and not acknowledged. His money went for his drinking. The Irish malady.

They were friendly enough but had a restrained, cold aura. We didn't see much of him, as he stayed upstairs in his bedroom when we visited. He was certainly very withdrawn emotionally. Both were from Northern Ireland and I always wondered if that explained their reserved personalities. I do know that they were "Orange" Protestant and definitely anti-Catholic, part of the Irish schism that has lasted for generations.

In spite of the problems, they were more sophisticated than our other relatives. Later, during my early teens, I did get close to Dad's sister, Aunt Ella. She was always my favorite, and a lady through and through. Very dignified and refined. There was a strong resemblance to her mother, white hair, fine features, and a successful businesswoman.

At that time I was 11, going into the 6th grade. I attended James Russell Lowell school, made new friends, and life was good. I was discovering boys and falling in love. What a rush that can be! A Valentine's Day card could be dreamed into a marriage proposal, white picket fence and life lived happily ever after. There was one boy who lived quite a distance away from me, but I would traipse across town just to walk by his house, heart pounding at the very thought he just might come out and see me.

As I recall, that one ended up in Juvenile Hall.

# Part II

# The Great Depression

## Black Thursday

The stock market crash occurred on October 24, 1929. Black Thursday, as it came to be known, created financial chaos. People stormed the banks to withdraw their savings. Men jumped from buildings on Wall Street. Fear and panic prevailed. During the following years, the economy spiraled downhill and unemployment rose rapidly. Familiar sights were men on street corners selling apples and pencils, begging for help. *"Brother, Can You Spare a Dime?"* became our theme song.

—    —    —

In 1931 we moved from 19th street to Olney, in North Philadelphia. Dad was working for the Klemm Electric Supply Company and, in spite of the Depression, was doing well. We bought a brand-new small row house on Fern Street. It was a much nicer environment for us and we were delighted to be able to live in what felt to us an "upper class" neighborhood. By 1934, however, Dad joined the ranks of the unemployed when his company went bankrupt. He lost his spirit and never got it back. It was necessary for us to move, as we were unable to stay in our house without Dad's income. At the time I was 14 and in junior high school, a young adult.

## Our Solution for Survival

Mother contacted her Aunt Rene (short for Irene) who was a wealthy widow. At that time, when we were desperate and turned to her for help, she had four empty, run-down houses in Collingswood, New Jersey. She agreed to allow us to move into one of the houses for $25 a month, with the understanding that we'd repair and clean all four of them. Earlier, the Presbyterian Church adjacent to the four houses had wanted to buy them from Aunt Rene. She removed all of her tenants, believing the arrangement was solid, but the deal fell through. In anger, she simply boarded the houses up and let them remain vacant. She ranted and raved for years about the dirty deal the church gave her. The one we moved into, 840 Maple Avenue, was our home for many years.

—    —    —

The move to New Jersey was traumatic. To us as teenagers, it meant leaving old friends, the neighborhood, the school we attended, the house we lived in, and everything familiar. We experienced a lot of fear and frustration. Our security had been taken away. We went along with the decision, of course; we had no choice. Like it or not, New Jersey was our destination.

We moved during the month of July after the end of the school year, and the cleaning and painting adventure began. Aunt Rene, her brother John Bommerschein, and Rene's handyman, Harold, arrived from Philadelphia with mops, brooms, buckets, old rags, paint, and brushes. What a trio they were!

## Aunt Rene

My Aunt Rene was quite a character – I must tell you more about her! She had buck teeth and terrible breath, and her body had a moldy, stale aura that was unpleasant. I tried to avoid direct contact with her. Her hair was dyed a reddish-brown,and she wore it arranged in a loose, scraggly bun. Her eyeglasses hung from a chain around her neck. In stark contrast to her untidy appearance, a huge diamond ring and wedding band adorned her left hand. She carried her purse pinned to her girdle. When she needed cash, up came the dress and slip and she dug around in the hidden purse. It didn't matter where she was, a store, restaurant, wherever.

When she was a young girl, she had married a wealthy older man, Will Eldridge, who owned property in Philadelphia and New Jersey. He had a home in Cape May, at the New Jersey shore. He must have had a boat of some sort. In the only picture I ever saw of him, after he was gone, he was decked out in the traditional white pants, navy blazer, and captain's hat. He was a good-looking man, with an aristocratic appearance, accented by pure white hair and a white mustache.

Will died when I was abut 10 years old. Aunt Rene got into psychic readings, seances, and trying to contact the departed. She was sure his spirit was with her, and I heard that Rene slept at the foot of their bed from them on, to be sure he would have enough room. When eating with us, she insisted we set a place at the table for Will.

We set our tables when we had company, even during the Depression, with linen table covers, silver (always kept spotlessly polished) and fine china and crystal. Will's place was always at the head of table. So there he was, in that empty chair, with us at every meal.

Before the Depression, we occasionally visited her. She lived in what was then considered an upscale neighborhood. The house was on a corner, and was quite large. Inside, the rooms were dark, the windows covered with heavy draperies that were kept closed. The living room was crowded with plush, oversized furniture, antique lamps, china figurines, and marble statues. We were never allowed to even sit in that room, just in the kitchen. No doubt her things were worth a fortune, but to me it looked and felt like a museum stuffed into a small space. It was claustrophobic; I felt stifled and not at all welcome.

Children weren't her favorite people. She ignored our existence whenever possible. Instructions from Mother were for us to be quiet, obedient, helpful, and polite. It was very intimidating to be in Rene's presence. One bit of wisdom which she shared frequently with us gives you an idea of what she was like: when we went on a vacation or to visit someone, she relished telling us how bad we were going to feel when we had to leave to come home.

The bottom line for Mother was that Aunt Rene had money and we needed help, so we had to be nice. That meant doing and being whatever the Queen desired. If she said jump, we were to ask, *"How high?"* How we hated it!

Lunch was a nightmare. It was mandatory that we sit at our dining room table and participate in the meal as a group. I tried not to be there mentally or emotionally. I didn't even want to look at any of them. In fact, I didn't dare look at my brother, who always made faces and made me giggle, which meant immediate dismissal from the table for me. Jim had that effect on me and he loved getting me in trouble.

Uncle John was elderly, with white hair, a ruddy complexion, and stocky build. He was a kind but cold and intimidating man. He always had a glass of water for his false teeth on the table right by his plate. If I looked in his direction, those teeth seemed to jump right out at me.

Harold, the handyman, was younger and slim, with sandy hair and watery blue eyes. He didn't say much, just worked hard and melted into the background. He was friendly to us, which we appreciated under the circumstances. Later, I learned that Harold was more than just Aunt Rene's handyman. He lived in her attic and took care of all of her needs.

In 1936 Rene died of syphilis in a mental hospital. That just might have had something to do with her mental state. Where and how she got it, I really don't know, nor do I want to. My brother visited her toward the end of her life. He told us that the radiator in her room was noisy. When he asked Aunt Rene if the noise bothered her, she replied, *"Be quiet - it's the only thing they're not charging me for."*

—   —   —

It took us several months to get rid of the accumulated dirt and grime on

Helen at age 13.

In the Drum and Bugle Corps.

Our house at 840 Maple Avenue in Collingswood, New Jersey (our unit on left).

the four houses. We had to scrub and paint every inch. Jim and I were sure those houses were haunted. We found many strange things. In the attic of one house, there was weird painting all over the floor. It appeared to us some sort of secret code. Another time, when we were cleaning a cellar in one of the houses, we pulled a leg out from under the stairs. Scared us to death. We thought we'd discovered a body. It turned out to be somebody's old wooden leg.

The houses were located on Maple Avenue, which ran parallel to the main street in town. They were two large, two-story duplexes, each having an attic and basement. The living room, dining room, kitchen, pantry, and a small back porch were on the first floor. The second floor contained four bedrooms and one large bathroom. Mother and Dad slept in the largest bedroom in the rear. I had a small room next to the bathroom at the top of the stairs. Jim had the front bedroom.

We couldn't afford to buy coal for the furnace in the basement, so the big old black wood-burning kitchen stove was our only source for heat. We cooked and baked on it intuitively, as there were no timers or specific settings for heat. A lot of time was spent around the table in the kitchen.

This was a warm, cozy atmosphere for sharing and eating. In the winter, Jim and I brought our nightclothes to the kitchen and warmed them by the fire before putting them on. Then we made a mad dash upstairs to our ice-cold beds with blankets that felt heavy as iron. It took a while for our body heat to make it comfortable enough to fall asleep. Even to this day, I sleep better with weight on me. It gives me a feeling of security.

It just occurred to me that I still use those old tricks. In the winter I enjoy putting my flannel night gown and robe in the clothes dryer. I strip naked while they are heating, then slide them over my cold body. What a glorious sensation. Pathetic in a way to resort to this for a thrill – I can only say wait until you reach 85, then you'll understand! I get my kicks where I can.

Two metal washtubs and the coal bin for the furnace were located in the basement. We had a two-burner gas heater and an old washing machine with rollers attached which we cranked by hand to wring out the laundry. Mother heated water in a huge metal container and used a smaller pot with a handle to transfer the water into the washing machine. After washing and running the clothes through the rollers, they went to the tubs for the rinse and were once again run through the rollers.

The next step was contingent on the weather. If it was raining or snowing, we hung the laundry on lines in the basement. If not, the wet laundry was carried up the basement steps in large baskets to be hung with clothespins on lines in the yard. It was my job to go out in freezing weather and pull the frozen laundry off the lines, and bring the clothes into the house to thaw. What a production! We did this every Monday. Tuesday was ironing day. That routine never changed.

Lack of a hot water heater necessitated that we carry kettles up to the bathroom for our baths. We soaked in the tub once a week in the winter. We took what Dad inelegantly referred to as "whore baths" in between. In those days we had to wear our clothes until they were really dirty.

Toys were few and far between in those days, so we treasured the ones we got. I still have a beautiful antique doll named Bertha that belonged to my mother. Her head is porcelain, and the features of her face exquisite: big blue eyes, long lashes, small nose and ruby lips turned up in a slight smile. The doll has brownish-red hair similar to Aunt Rene's, gathered at the back with curls falling from it. The hair has been thoroughly cleaned and rearranged several times over the years. She was made in Germany, with a wooden torso and jointed arms, legs, hands and feet. She is about two and a half feet tall. She is presently on a stand in a glass enclosure, dressed in a lovely white outfit, and looks just marvelous.

## Family Dynamics

I was fourteen when I started the ninth grade. My brother, Jim, was seventeen and a junior in high school. Although there were three years difference in our ages, we were only two years apart in school. Because of my December birthday, I started first grade a year early, and Jim was held back a year along the way. While he was always the more intelligent one of the family, he had a behavior problem in the eighth grade. His main difficulty was not showing up for classes.

My brother had so much natural talent. He played piano and guitar by ear and was a champion at table tennis, as well as court tennis. He was also very good looking - six feet tall, and well-built, with slightly wavy brown hair, blue eyes, and freckles. Eventually, he attended Bucknell University, where he earned an electrical engineering degree.

Even though Jim had all the brains and abilities, his shortcoming was that he disliked most people and showed it. He seemed more comfortable in his own intellectual world. Jim could turn on the charm when he chose to, but could also shut others out at will.

He could dance gracefully and well. When Mother wanted Jim to give me tennis lessons or teach me how to dance, it was obvious to me that he didn't want to. The short dancing lesson in our living room ended with his side remark to Mom, *"It's like trying to push a Mack truck around."*

He took me out just one time on the tennis court. After a few volleys back and forth, with me not even being able to get the ball over the net, Jim said, *"Forget it, kid, you'll never be able to play."* After that, I never did. I felt awkward, unable to do anything athletic. So much for brotherly love.

There was never any contest between Jim and me; Mother doted on him. I have always maintained my brother was an only child. He knew he was in the Number One position and there was no way for me to combat it. A few times we had fun and laughed together, but mostly he lived a separate life. Later in life I gained some self-confidence. During my high school years, I was insecure and low on self-esteem. Going through the teenage years was difficult, to say the least. I would cry and not know why, giggle uncontrollably at stupid events or things. I usually felt that I did not fit in.

—     —     —

Mom was a good-looking woman of medium build, with brown hair and brown eyes. She always insisted she had Indian blood. She did have olive skin, but I suspect she wanted to be something she wasn't. Every afternoon, she retired to her bed for exactly one half hour for a rest. Then she would wash up and put on a fresh housedress

She was a good cook and kept an immaculate house. Mom would empty an ashtray before you finished smoking a cigarette. Once a week, using a bucket of warm water and soft rags, she got on her hands and knees and cleaned all of the floors, including the large wooden stairway. We could have literally eaten off the floor.

I swore to myself that when I had a home it would not be so rigid and perfect. It seemed to me that Mom thrived on being praised for her cooking, her spotlessly clean house, and her talent for entertaining.

Mother had a delicious sense of humor and could always see the funny side of life. When she went shopping on Haddon Avenue she came back with stories that made our sides ache from giggling. The one I remember most is once when she went to buy produce. An old man started chatting with her and invited her to his home to see his pea vine. He kept insisting the pea vine that he had was special. We always wondered what she would have seen if she had risked the trip. She was friendly to everyone.

20

The routine in our home was set in concrete. We were assigned chores and did them or else. I helped Mom with housecleaning. Jim took care of the trash and kept his room clean. We shared kitchen duty every other night, until Mom bribed Jim with freedom from that duty in exchange for attending school and getting passing grades. Guess who did the dishes after that?

Mom was definitely the head of our family, and could be very difficult to please. Dad always went along with whatever Mom wanted or said. We all did. If not, we got the silent treatment that could last for weeks. My feeling about her was that she wanted to have money and, since we didn't, she was dissatisfied with her lot in life. Money was her first priority, followed by Jim, maybe Dad, and me on the tail end. She cultivated friendships with moneyed friends and relatives. We came after she paid homage to them. I resented being so far down in the pecking order.

The ironic part is she never got any of their fortunes. Aunt Rene and all of the others passed away and left her zilch. In a way, I felt justice was done. In my eyes, her motives were selfish and morally bankrupt.

Mother had a strong personality and was always in control of any family activities. Whether it was a visit to other relatives, a picnic in a park, a trip to the Shore or a big family dinner at home, she planned the menu, when and where we were to go and when we were to come home. For some reason, everyone connected to her went along with it. No one want to face the consequences of her disapproval if they should object or try to change the plans.

I handled it all by being obedient and taking easy courses in school so I would be assured of good grades. I sought approval and acceptance outside the family, and just existed as best I could while at home.

Actually, I was a bit of a wimp to go along with the treatment I received, but it was the easy way out. In those days, we didn't know how to be assertive. Even if we'd known, we wouldn't have dared.

Dad dealt with this by sitting in his favorite chair, reading or listening to the radio. It was his island of privacy where he could shut Mom out. I had many conflicting feelings regarding the way she treated Dad. She belittled him in subtle ways. He was perfect in my eyes. He was a tall, easy-going, good-looking Irishman. I always felt he was the one in the family who loved me and was on my side. He had a charming personality, was squeaky clean, and smelled grand at all times. Until the Depression, he was a successful lighting salesman, and sold the lighting for some of the high-rise buildings in Philadelphia. Once, he took us up on the roof of a skyscraper to show us the sign he sold that read PSFS (the Philadelphia Saving Fund Society). In those days, we didn't have that many skyscrapers, so that was quite a thrill.

Dad was willing to do anything to provide for us. He pumped gas, sat in model houses, and worked as a salesman in various retail stores. No matter what, we always had a roof over our heads and food on the table. He developed colon cancer and left us at the age of 69. This seems so young to me now. His untimely death has forced me to pay attention to this particular health problem. I've had the dubious pleasure of submitting to colonoscopies regularly for the past twenty years. The night before the procedure will always keep my humility intact.

Mom had a way of putting me down by saying, *"You are just like your Aunt Margaret and Aunt Hazel."* Because I knew she disliked both of them, it was clear that she felt the same about me. Aunt Hazel was her step-sister, and she could do nothing right in Mom's eyes. Aunt Margaret was my father's younger sister. She was glamorous and successful. All of her undies, nightgowns, and robes were of luxurious heavy satin and lace. I remember watching her iron them to perfection and wishing some day that I could own and wear garments like those. Mother criticized her constantly for wasting her money, but I was intrigued by her and her life style.

Mother hung on until she was one hundred and one. She did quite well until the last ten years - good genes, no doubt. In my eyes, her character defects became more and more obvious in her later years. She was impossible to please. No matter what the family did for her, it was never enough. For me personally, I had to give up trying to gain her approval and just do the best I could. The bottom line is that she, no doubt, also did the best she could. My regret is that I never really got close to her, and she really did not know me. Painful, but true.

### Food in Our Town

Collingswood, a typical small town, sported beautiful tree-lined streets. The main street, Haddon Avenue, was where we went for all of our marketing, movies, and social life.

I can still smell the aroma of garlic, fresh breads, and spices that permeated that small area. I remember the wooden floors, glass-front cases with the goodies on display, and shelves along the wall filled with interesting food.

A far cry from the sterile, over-packaged foods found in today's supermarkets.

Many small grocery stores and delicatessens carried lunch meats such as pepper beef, Taylor's pork roll, dried beef, and boiled ham. Our favorite after-school snack was kosher pickles, stored in wooden barrels, and bulk potato chips. During the spring and summer, our local produce stores carried corn right from the fields, tomatoes fresh off the vine, and peaches direct from the orchard. Their flavor was beyond compare.

Local bakeries sold crumb cake, a fancy cake called Charlotte Russe with a delicious cream filling served in a paper cup, and cinnamon buns that we called sticky buns. There was no stinting on butter, cream, eggs, or sugar in those days. We'd never heard of cholesterol, much less low or non-fat foods, or artificial sweeteners. Little wonder we had weight problems!

At school during recess, men with carts came to the playground with hot pretzels, loaded with salt and mustard. The carts were rickety, made of wood with big wheels for mobility. There was a hot compartment in the front to keep the pretzels warm. What a welcome sight for us, especially on icy cold days! The pretzels that are available in the malls and theaters today don't compare to the ones we had.

I was raised with the notion that it was mandatory to feed guests. Cold cuts, bread, and coffee cake were brought out no matter what time of the day or evening.

In spite of the shortage of money, our family enjoyed great food. Mother was a good cook and could whip up a tasty cinnamon topped cake without eggs and just a dab of butter. At times she would add raisins for variety. We also raised tomatoes in our back yard. They were our main staple one summer. Mom served them fried, stewed, and sliced.

Cabbage in all forms was a frequent meal. I happened to like it and Mother told me how lucky this was for me, since I could always eat, even if I were poor. Like that was good news? Brisket, ham or corned beef went well with it. At times mother boiled it with vinegar. A cut-glass cruet of vinegar sat on the table at all times. We put vinegar in stew, soup, anything that needed a little "kick."

I think that came from either the Irish or Dutch side of the family. We were definitely mongrels: English, Irish, Dutch and who knows what else.

I still use some of Mom's recipes. I enjoy macaroni and cheese made with bacon, tomatoes, onion, and sharp cheese. We had that with creamed chipped beef. Other nights, we had stewed tomatoes and mashed potatoes. As a meat substitute, we had fried eggplant. Omelets made a good dinner.

Our snacks after school consisted of a slice of white bread covered with molasses, ketchup, mayonnaise, tomato or onion. It's funny what can seem yummy when you're young and hungry. Was our food that much better, or is it just the memory and youth that make it seem so?

One summer we discovered we had a cherry tree in the back yard. Jim and I climbed up and proceeded to eat them. Mother came out and told us to gather some for her and she'd bake a pie. About ten minutes later she came running out of the house screaming, *"Stop, don't eat any more! They're full of worms!"* We'd been devouring worms for about an hour! To this day I never eat a cherry without splitting it in half and checking it carefully.

## School Days

Collingswood High School was a stately old stone and brick structure, located on Collings Avenue across from Knight's Park. It had three stories with a basement that housed a few classrooms as well as the boys' and girls' lockers and bathrooms. An auditorium and the staff offices were located on the first floor, while the second and third floors consisted of classrooms. There was the usual gymnasium, and a football field with a new stadium.

Knight's Park, located in the center of town, was surrounded by lovely homes. The more affluent folk, including the mayor, resided in this section of town. The park was quite large, with a lake, walks, magnificent trees, and well-kept grassy areas. It had a hockey field, and during the winter the lake froze over and was perfect for ice-skating.

After school, we gathered under a tree to rehash the day, make plans for activities, and complain about school. We also gossiped a lot about boys, discussing who did or didn't have a date for the football game, movies, or the Saturday dance. The boys we were interested in were the "jocks," who later turned out to not necessarily be the best choices. The "nerds" were the ones who became the most successful.

Our social life consisted mainly of hanging out in one of the two local drug stores. Each had marble-topped, old-fashioned soda fountain counters, and ice cream tables with wrought-iron chairs. The pharmacies were located in the rear.

Another place to congregate was a little store called "Tak-a-Boost", where we could get a drink by that name for five cents. We stayed there for hours on end, smoking cigarettes, chatting and giggling. (Why do teenage girls giggle so much? Insecurity?)

We thought we were so cool. High-backed booths in the rear of the room provided the perfect place for us clandestine smokers to hide from the passers-by on Haddon Avenue. The Tak-a-Boost drink was a sweet, iced tea concoction served with a pretzel on the side. The amazing thing about this drink is that it was actually made up of tonics and medicines, with some caffeine to pep it up. It originated in Riverside, New Jersey in 1913.

Most of us were poor, so on Saturday one of us would buy a ticket for the matinee at the local theater. After entering, the person with the ticket casually went to one of the curtained exits and let the rest of us sneak in, one at a time. I honestly think the manager knew what we were up to and looked the other way.

—     —     —

During heavy snow in winter, we went sledding on a token "hill." In good weather, we used this same hill for roller-skating. That part of New Jersey is flat, and hills are few and far between. Kids participated in the usual sports activities – football, soccer, baseball, basketball, and hockey. School itself was relatively easy, although I did get thrown out of biology when I cried about having to dissect a frog. I also dropped out of typing class, but later earned my living by typing.

As stated previously, I switched to easy business courses and breezed through them. The one teacher that stands out in my mind was our English instructor, Miss Marsden. She taught us basic Latin and read Shakespeare in a way that I could understand.

I had a crush on the captain of the football team, who was dating the head cheerleader. Ziggy, a real jock of a soccer player, looked really good to me but I never dared get near him. That seemed to be the theme of my life as a teenager - always wanted the one I couldn't get.

I joined the Drum and Bugle Corps to get into the games for free. We were given the choice of learning to play the bugle or beating the drum. Not being musically talented, I had no choice but to fake it with the drum.

Our uniforms consisted of a long white skirt, white blouse, a white pullover sweater, and a navy and gold cape, topped off by a military-style hat. We wore saddle shoes and bobby socks. Not glamorous, but practical.

I slopped trays in the school cafeteria to get a free lunch. My main duty was to stand behind a counter where the students piled their dirty trays. I dumped off the garbage into a large can and stacked the trays.

We had good homemade food, and the ladies who worked there treated us with kindness. They gave us lots of special goodies, my favorite being a huge oatmeal cookie with about an inch of real whipped cream slathered on top.

During that period I wore hand-me-downs from my Aunt Hazel. They were mostly black crepe dresses and not at all appropriate for school. This was humiliating, but the majority of my friends were in the same boat. We were all poor and struggling to get along, so we did whatever was necessary to survive.

—  —  —

Some of the students came from wealthy families. My closest friend, Mary, lived by Knight's Park and was one of the more financially secure individuals at school. Her father was a well-known lawyer. She was a vivacious redhead with naturally curly hair, blue eyes, freckles, and a great body. Her activities included hockey and the Drum and Bugle Corps. She had a sense of humor similar to Joan Rivers' style.

Her family allowed her the use of one of the family cars occasionally. She shared this privilege and gave us rides. It was sheer luxury for us, and we did have good times driving around town and showing off.

One summer day, Mary jammed about eight of us into her family sedan and drove us out to the country. We went to a cranberry bog (New Jersey is flat and low, so we did have those) to go swimming. The bog was located down in a hollow - out of sight, we thought - and decided to go skinny-dipping. The water was relatively shallow and warm, and the bushes tickled our bodies. The freedom of nakedness was a new, pleasant sensation.

After about an hour of running around and splashing in the water, one of the girls looked up and saw a police car above. The sight of that car created chaos. We all ran for our clothes, screaming. We imagined we would be arrested, but the car just drove out of the area when they realized we had seen them. There is no doubt in my mind that they thoroughly enjoyed the sights and it was the talk of the police station for quite some time. Our biggest fear was that our parents would find out. Ours was a prudish society.

—  —  —

When I turned fifteen, I learned how to drive. We could get a learner's permit at that age and a license at sixteen. Dad, Uncle Charlie, and Jim all took turns trying to teach me to drive a car with a clutch and four gears. One by one, they gave up in frustration.

My friend, Mary, volunteered to teach me. She came to our house in her dad's car, and away we went. All was going well until she decided to take me to one of our few hills to teach me how to park. Why she thought I needed to learn to park on a hill at that stage of my learning, I'll never know.

I lost control and rolled backward down the hill and hit a tree at the bottom. At that point, Mary gave up and took me home. All the way home, she kept reassuring me that I was a good driver. Later, I heard that when her mother asked how I'd done, Mary replied, *"Just fine."* Then she fainted.

—    —    —

It's hard to believe, but we had sororities and fraternities back then. They were cliques and a bit snobby. I was truly surprised when invited to join one of the bigger and more desirable ones, the "tri-delts" or Delta Delta Delta. That did a lot to help my poor self-image. The sorority had the usual "rushing" and then the initiation. They had bi-weekly meetings (mostly gossip sessions) that were held in different homes. The girls were all popular, and I was in awe that I had been included in the group.

I vividly remember two sisters who I thought were beautiful. The younger sister had red hair and a bubbly personality. The older one, Peggy, had hair so black that it had blue tints in it. She wore it long in a pageboy style. There I was, with light brown naturally curly hair, longing for that straight style. It was my idea at the time that glamour had a lot to do with straight hair. I was very insecure back then, and wished my looks were different, not appreciating what nature had given me.

Once a year we went to the Norton Hotel in Atlantic City for a convention. It took a lot of talking to persuade my parents to allow me to go. I was afraid my brother Jim would tell them how raucous it would be. All the boys from school coincidentally showed up the same weekend. Hanging out on the deck in front of the hotel overlooking the ocean was great. It was beautiful day or night, so we spent a lot of time out there.

—    —    —

One of the girls in our school, Maria, was the daughter of a very rich Italian family, supposedly in the import-export business. She came to high school in a blue Cadillac convertible. How I lusted after that car and swore some day I'd have one. Maria wore a fur coat to school in the winter, and the gossip was that she was naked under it. She never took it off, so who knows.

To fit in, it was necessary to wear a long brown skirt, a fitted suede jacket, saddle shoes, white angora bobby socks, and angora earmuffs. Eventually, I was able to eke out the money for this popular outfit. It still amuses me that teenagers want so desperately to be different, yet always dress identically.

On weekends, we wore riding clothes complete with jodhpurs, a jacket and a riding crop. We would go to a park by Cooper River, which ran adjacent to our area, walk around, play with our dog (if we had one), and try to look like we'd just returned from the stable. We never got near a horse, let alone rode one, but the few rich pupils at school did, so I suppose we wanted everyone to think we did too.

Over the years, some of that group have gotten together for reunions. We call ourselves the Golden Girls. We wonder how we ever thought we were fooling anybody with that performance, or why we wanted to.

## Employment

This was a difficult period of time. To eat and pay the rent, we all had to work. Dad got a job pumping gas. Mom went to work darning linens for a company her brother managed. The company supplied aprons, tablecloths, etc., for restaurants in Philadelphia. My brother delivered papers. I lied about my age (I was fifteen) and went to work at Woolworth's Five-and-Dime store. I didn't do too well. They put me in the toy department at Christmas time, and I had difficulty wrapping the large unwieldy stuff.

After Woolworth's, I got jobs as a waitress and soda jerk, and was not much good at either of them. I got fired from the waitress job for telling a customer to lay off the duck on the menu. It was green with mold.

The problem that I had as a soda jerk seemed to be that I was prone to give my friends too much ice cream in their shakes and sodas. I got myself fired from a local ice cream shop as well as one of the drug stores.

Our area of New Jersey raised great tomatoes, and huge quantities of them. Campbell's Soup in Camden hired local high school kids in the summer to work during the tomato harvest. My experience there was also sad. First I worked in a large warehouse, where the tomatoes rolled by on huge, moving belts. We stood on wet wooden slats and had to be quick to spot the bad ones and pick them off. I couldn't keep up, so they transferred me to the canning department.

There they had large machines that automatically poured the soup into the cans. From there the cans traveled around a narrow circular channel, past the operator, to a machine where lids were mechanically attached.

We stood near the machine with a pitcher of soup to add to unfilled cans. If they were too low, we had to pluck them off the belt as they went by. We also re-filled lids in our individual machines. They were kept across the room in stacks of at least 100. We would scoop them up with two hands from the wall, cross the room and insert them in a slot at our machine.

I received early retirement because more than once I dropped the lids, and cut myself on a can when trying to pick it off the belt as it went by. It was humiliating to be a washout at Campbell's.

My brother worked there, too. He came home one night telling us that a boy named Clarence, who was obese, sweaty, and unattractive, to say the least, had fallen into a vat of tomato juice that was about to be canned. They never told the management. We avoided buying tomato juice for several years to make sure that batch was gone.

—    —    —

After school, my duties included cleaning the house and getting dinner ready. We always had fish on Friday, since it was fresh that day at the market. The first time I prepared fish, I didn't salt it, figuring it came out of salt water and wouldn't need it. That debacle was just one more episode that my family never let me forget, such as the time I accidentally locked myself in a clothes closet, and had to wait hours to be let out by a gloating brother.

## Following the Depression

In 1937, I graduated from high school. I was seventeen, ready to go out into the world and work. The worst years of the Depression were behind us. Dad was working for Gulf Oil & Gas Company checking local service stations for cleanliness and efficiency.

We had taken in a boarder, a young man named Johnny, who worked in Philadelphia. Mom put him in the small room in the front by Jim. Johnny paid Mom $15 a week for the room, laundry service, and meals. He didn't do too well managing money and usually borrowed at least $10 of his rent back by mid-week. He was twenty-one at the time; two years older than my brother. Johnny partied at times and was fun when tipsy. When he would come home from a party, he would try to sneak up to his room but he never made it. Mom always caught him, much to his chagrin.

He never crossed the line around me. In fact, he treated me better than Jim did. Mother, Dad, and Jim might not be home for the evening, but Johnny made sure to be home early so I wouldn't be alone in the house. He was the only one who cared enough to be there for me.

Jim decided to delay going to college for at least a year to save up enough money to enroll, and after he graduated from high school he went to work full-time at Campbell's. He paid my tuition to a small business school in Collingswood taught by Mrs. MacNeil in her home. I walked to her house from Maple Avenue. Mary, my friend from high school, took the course with me, along with a few other girls we knew.

—      —      —

Mrs. MacNeil was a tall, thin, angular woman. She had natural red hair, wore glasses and had pale blue eyes. She was businesslike and strict, but congenial. It was hard work, but the surroundings were enjoyable. Gregg shorthand was taught in the living room, and typing was taught in the dining room. There were fifteen desks with Underwood typewriters. The course ran for three months and gave me the skills I needed for office work.

After graduating, I went to work at Mohrfeld's, a local coal and oil heating company in Collingswood a few blocks from my house. I walked to work. Mohrfeld's was owned by two brothers.

The older one, Carl, was short and well-built, slightly balding, and average looking. He was the quiet, serious type. The employees didn't fool around when he was in the office. Herb was the younger brother; tall, thin, and good-looking. He was the heating engineer and was light-hearted and always joking.

—      —      —

The coal was delivered to Mohrfeld's by train. The weight scale was next to the office building, which was a two-story wood frame building adjacent to the railroad tracks. The coal receptacles and parking for delivery trucks were around back. In the beginning, I worked downstairs in the coal department with Mildred, who was friendly and easy to be with.

Mildred was a middle-aged old maid with faded, reddish brown hair and blue eyes. She was old-fashioned, even for those days. The drivers and Carl called her Miss Mortimer. Herb called her "Red." It was easy to see who was her favorite - she lit up when Herb was around.

I was paid $10 a week until I was promoted to secretary for Herb six months later. My salary was raised to $12 a week and I moved upstairs to the oil-heating department. Between living at home and taking my lunch to work, I was doing pretty well.

—      —      —

My typewriter was located on a stand by a window overlooking the railroad tracks. A cat came by every morning. He sat by the side of the tracks, and just before a train came speeding by, he would make a dash across in front of it. It fascinated me to watch this game. One morning, though, his timing was off. It was a sad day for me, and even worse for the cat.

## Raging Hormones

During this period I was working and dating a guy ten years my senior. Wally was of Scottish descent – tall, with sky-blue eyes, sandy hair, and full lips. His first love was golf, followed closely by partying. We spent a lot of time together at a local country club. Wally played golf and I stayed in the "19th hole" playing the pinball machines, darts, and dice games with the bartender.

Wally's father was a well-known creator of handmade golf clubs. One of his customers was Bing Crosby. Wally had his father make me a personal club with the hope of getting me interested in the sport. It didn't work.

–      –      –

In those days, the idea of having sex was extremely tempting. After all, at that age our hormones were at their peak and raging. What it was "really like" was an intriguing mystery. We didn't hear much about the risk of getting diseases.

–      –      –

I got into some heavy petting during my high school years, but I was always too terrified to "go all the way." Boys would say anything to try to convince me that it would be okay. I remember how they insisted they were in intense pain to try to make me feel guilty about stopping. I just knew I'd get pregnant and my life would be ruined. I knew a few girls in high school who were shipped out of town to a distant relative's home to have their "illegitimate" baby, to avoid disgracing the family.

–      –      –

Sex entered my life with Wally. I really loved him. It didn't happen often, but we did manage a few interludes. We used the cabin in the woods where we had our parties.

–      –      –

That is more than you need to know about my sexual activity during my late teens and early twenties. It was a totally different time, and society's moral codes were much more restrictive, but we were human, and we had the same sex drive that young people have had throughout history. A lot of action took place in parked cars and behind barns, I can guarantee that!

## Philly

In those days, it was a big deal on Saturday or Sunday to go across the Delaware River to Philadelphia. On Saturday, we shopped in Wanamaker's or Strawbridge & Clothier. Sometimes we walked around the business district, and snooped through the hotel lobbies. Walnut and Chestnut were two of the more elegant streets, relatively narrow and paved with brick. Chestnut Street housed the expensive stores and hotels, as well as prestigious business offices.

When we could afford it, we ate lunch at one of the nicer restaurants, such as Wanamaker's tearoom. We met there under the eagle, a huge bronze statue on a platform on the first floor, where we sat and waited for friends.

It was indeed grand in those days. There was a feeling of underlying cosmic energy; compared to our small town, it felt much more active and alive. Everyone dressed up – hats, gloves, suits - very chic and cosmopolitan. Linen, crystal and silver on all dining tables. Nothing casual, all quite formal.

– – –

Philadelphia is the heart and birthplace of American Independence. The Betsy Ross House, Independence Hall, and the Liberty Bell are all there. The statue of William Penn is in the center of the city, perched atop City Hall. We had the history of that great man crammed into our heads from the cradle. Benjamin Franklin was another famous character we learned a lot about – perhaps more than we wanted to know.

The Mummers' New Year's Day parade was a spectacle I will always remember with great fondness. The string bands were all from South Philadelphia. They wore magnificent costumes with lots of feathers and glitter and strutted down Broad Street. It could be bitter cold, but they warmed our very heart and soul. I loved them then and still do.

In those days, my goals were to attend the Army-Navy game and someday go to New York City and get a job there. That's about as far into the future as I could conceive.

## *"The Jersey Bounce"*

On weekends we went to the local roadhouses. All of them were out of town since Collingswood was a "dry" community. This would usually be our group of close girl friends from school. How we got away with hanging out in the bars and drinking beer is a mystery, but we did. Mostly we just danced and socialized. It was a matter of bar-hopping to catch the action or the guys we were secretly looking for.

We had favorites: Cinelli's, a restaurant and bar that served excellent spaghetti, the Log Cabin, the Old Tavern, and the Loran House that served grilled shrimp. That odor permeated the whole place.

We had a lot of Saturday night parties in different homes. We always went to a house where there was a piano and spent the evening gathered around it singing.

For some unknown reason, our group of girls started getting involved with boys from Haddon Heights, a small town nearby. We met them in the bars. Apparently they were more exciting than the boys we knew from high school, because they were out-of-towners.

—     —     —

Occasionally, we pooled our money, rented a cabin out in the woods, and got a keg of beer. We went back again on Sunday afternoon to finish the beer and clean up. That was my favorite time because there were fewer of us and it was more casual and relaxed. That pretty much took care of the entire weekend.

During summer vacation, two or three of us rented an apartment or a room in Ocean City, which was also a dry city. At times we crossed the bridge to Sommer's Point where the bars were and the action was.

We spent all day on the beach, sunning and swimming. Hot dogs and hamburgers taste better with sand and surf, and we consumed a lot of them. Strolling on the boardwalk (referred to as the boards) was another favorite pastime. Taylor's pork roll sandwiches and salt-water taffy were local treats, and under the boards was a good place to get out of the sun. At night it served to protect us from the public eye.

At times we went to Steele Pier in Atlantic City, known for shows that featured horses diving off a diving board into a pool with a rider on their back. We once met and talked to the actor who played Rochester (Jack Benny's sidekick) out on the pier by the stage.

Big bands performed there, including Tommy and Jimmy Dorsey, Glenn Miller, Benny Goodman, and Tex Beneke. I remember hearing them play *"Moonlight Serenade," "Pennsylvania 6-5000," "The Jersey Bounce," "Let's Get Away From it All,"* and *"Green Eyes."* The list goes on and on. The music was marvelous, the dancing romantic and exciting. Swing, ballroom dancing, jitterbug – we did it all!

I loved Jack Leonard, who sang with Tommy Dorsey. His version of *"Marie"* was divine. Jack performed at a roadhouse called the Rustic Tavern. This happened to be the same spot where Frank Sinatra was later discovered. Leonard faded after the advent of the Sinatra craze. I feel truly blessed to have lived through that era. My music.

—    —    —

It was during these teenage years that my life-long passion began for the Chairman of the Board, Ol' Blue Eyes - Frank Sinatra. He has given me many hours of ecstasy, relaxing and immersing myself in the music he creat-ed. Years later, when I lived in Palm Springs, I happened to have the same hairdresser as Barbara Sinatra. When she heard about my loyalty and love for her husband, she brought me a signed photograph of him. I have a shrine in my bedroom with all of Sinatra's music on CDs and, of course, the photo of him. When I die, my kids have promised to have his hit *"I Did it My Way,"* played for me.

In the late '60s, Sinatra's pilot (an acquaintance of my husband) called us when he learned that the "Rat Pack" was going to be at the Sands Hotel in Las Vegas. We got tickets and flew there for the show. Wow, what a memo-rable night. I was sure Frank was singing just for me until I went to the ladies room and heard other women saying the same thing. What talent and charisma that man had! For decades my husband Chuck and I had an understanding. It would be okay if he slept with Elizabeth Taylor and I slept with Sinatra. That worked. We never had to test it.

—    —    —

On that same trip to Vegas, I went to the coffee shop in the Sands for lunch. A man at the adjoining table kept staring at me while I was chatting with the waitress. He stopped by my table and asked if I was from Philadelphia. I told him I was but that I'd been trying for years to get rid of the nasal twang I had acquired from that area. He laughed and remarked that he could still hear it. Afterward, the waitress told me that it was Joey Bishop.

Later in life, I had the good fortune to meet and become a friend of a gra-cious lady, Frances Adair. She is a typical southern lady, exuding charm and dignity. I feel honored to have her as a true friend. Frances was able to relate many glorious memories and has lived a full and magic life, rubbing elbows with the rich and famous. Her husband Tom was a well-known lyri-cist. He wrote many of Sinatra's hits and worked with Bing Crosby for sev-eral years. *"Let's Get Away from It All"* and *"Violets for Your Furs"* are two

34

The signed photo of Frank Sinatra given me by his wife, Barbara.

Here I am in my ocelot coat.

My first love, Wally.

My brother Jim.

examples of his music. Tom also wrote scripts for television sitcoms. *The Munsters, My Three Sons,* and *I Dream of Jeannie* were a few of them. In 1957, he was nominated for an Oscar.

—    —    —

All in all, my life was quite peaceful and satisfying up to December 7, 1941. Things had certainly improved greatly from the depths of the Depression. Living at home and surrounded by family and good friends, with a decent job and a fun social life, I really didn't have much to complain about.

# Part III

# World War II

*"Okay, Girls, Man Your Bunks!"*

## Pearl Harbor

Beginning in the late '30s, we began hearing news about trouble in Europe and Asia. Germany had annexed several countries, and Japan had invaded China. By 1941 much of the world was embroiled in war. The Germans had conquered much of Europe, nearly defeated Great Britain, were fighting the British in North Africa and Greece, and had attacked their former partner, driving deep into the Soviet Union. The Japanese were island-hopping all across the Pacific Ocean, and tensions were rising. Hirohito, Hitler, and Mussolini were names that were becoming all too familiar.

Up until that point, we'd managed to stay on our side of the pond, but the news on the radio and in the newspapers became more alarming with each passing day. War clouds were gathering and becoming darker, and we all wondered how much longer we could avoid being dragged into the war.

—       —               —

On December 7, 1941, I was in Philadelphia visiting friends. I was twenty-one, working as a stenographer in Mohrfeld's, still living at home in Collingswood, New Jersey. It was in the afternoon when we heard the news on the radio that Japan had attacked us at Pearl Harbor, and it put us all in a state of shock.

We didn't know for sure where Hawaii was, let alone why it would be bombed. We were confused and just wanted to get home. Those of us from New Jersey got back across the Delaware River Bridge as soon as possible. We had no idea of the impact this would have on our lives.

We stayed glued to our radios, waiting for more news. On Monday, President Roosevelt broadcast his famous "Day of Infamy" speech to Congress. Later, Germany and Italy declared war on the United States, and we declared war on them. The United States now belonged to the Allies, which consisted of Great Britain, France, the Soviet Union, China, and dozens of other countries. Japan, Germany, Italy and a few more formed the Axis.

## War!

As a country, we knew we were in trouble. We weren't prepared for this attack, and even less able to ward off further ones. Everyone understood it would take a lot of doing to fight back. Factories that had only recently recovered from the Depression were converted from making various con-

38

sumer goods to manufacturing airplanes, ammunition, communications equipment, uniforms – anything for the war effort. People were hired and trained to do the necessary jobs, and droves of young men enlisted in the Armed Forces. Rumors flew, submarines were sighted off both coasts, and blackouts and rationing began. We were definitely at war.

During this period, we were asked to give up our iron frying pans and save old grease for the war effort. Not to mention the tinfoil from chewing gum, and string which we wrapped in balls. Who knows whether they used any of this stuff, but it made us feel that we were doing something to help.

On a lighter note, one of the worst things that I think came about during the war years was horrendous stuff called margarine. Back then it was a white, lard-looking goo with a packet of yellow dye inside the package. We mixed in the yellow dye to make it resemble butter. Using margarine was a real sacrifice on my part, and I have never had it in my home since. I think anything tastes better with butter on it – real butter.

–       –       –

I quit my job at the coal and oil heating company and went to work at RCA (Radio Corporation of America) in Camden, as a stenographer for a group of four inventive engineers. Engineers are a breed of their own – in a different mental world from the rest of us. They were easy to work for as long as you typed the words they fed you. It was a whole new environment for me. They were working on submarine sonar and that sort of thing.

The work was all "Top Secret" and God knows it was safe with me! I had no idea what they were talking about. I just learned the words, transcribed, and typed them. I doubt they even knew what else I did with my time. I spent a lot of hours in the ladies' room when I was first hired, memorizing the lexicon and hiding when not busy.

We started to see more and more military. Even our little church in Collingswood had lost quite a few boys at Pearl Harbor. It was a sad time because we had known so many of them from high school.

Now that war had hit so close to home, it created a whole new attitude. Up until this point, we had taken our safety for granted, but all of a sudden we felt vulnerable. Would they attack again and take our country? Confusion and fear were with us on a daily basis. It was difficult to digest all the negative news, and it seemed almost like a nightmare to be living in the midst of it. It felt as though the whole world was being destroyed and it would take a miracle to stop it.

Patriotism was raging. Loyal Americans who happened to be of German or Italian descent came under suspicion overnight. Japanese-Americans had it the worst – many were incarcerated in camps. Fear and mistrust reigned.

My brother Jim left Bucknell University and enlisted in the Army Air Corps. While on leave, he met a girl on the beach in Ocean City, and it was love at first sight. Grace was ten years younger, petite and pretty.

She went back with him to his training base and they married there. Jim and Grace stayed together literally "til death did them part." Our generation was prone to take marriage vows to heart and be loyal and true to each other. We believed in the "for better or for worse" part of "as long as you both shall live." My personal feeling is that by working through their problems, couples of my generation enhanced their love for each other and as a result had a much lower divorce rate than we have now.

My mother felt she was losing control and didn't like it a bit. She'd lost her son to a girl ten years his junior, and I was in love with Wally, an older man. Mom was an expert at letting us know she disapproved of our choices, but at this stage of our lives we really didn't care. I think by then we were both aware there was no way we could please her.

During this period we were inundated with slogans like *"V for Victory," "Remember Pearl Harbor," "Loose lips sink ships,"* and the term *"Yellow Peril."* We were completely swept up in the flag-waving fanfare. We had Bond Rallies at RCA every week with bands playing and celebrities making speeches. I remember Carole Lombard being at one of them. It was an exciting time and the rallies touched every patriotic nerve of our young bodies.

–      –      –

I was very interested in going into the service, but was holding out for the Navy, because Dad had been a sailor during World War I. He served on a mine-sweeper operating outside of Philadelphia and usually came home on weekends. He was called "Philadelphia Jim" by his shipmates because there he was, serving his country, but able to go home frequently.

I had strong patriotic feelings and was willing to do anything to help the war effort. We were told if we joined the military, we'd free up a man for active duty. It made sense to me that we could really be of help. I was yearning to make something of myself, and if it took a war to do it, I was ready. I think we were all ready to do anything we could for our country.

–      –      –

Naturally, we were totally immersed in the news of the war. No television, but the radio, newspapers, and news reels that were shown in the movie theaters kept us informed. We heard stories of the bloody battles in places like the Philippines, Guadalcanal, and the Solomon Islands. Convoys of merchant ships were being attacked by German U-boats.

My memory of it is that the universe seemed to come alive with energy. We had a common goal as a country, and were all frightened, but we were strong and determined to fight back, no matter what it took.

—    —    —

When I was working at RCA, one of my friends and I wrote the following poem, dated May 12, 1942. If a Navy man were to read it today, especially the line about being "always gay," he would flip, I'm sure! Those were the days when gay actually meant happy. Now, I'm aware this is bad poetry and really corny, but we worked hard to compose it. It certainly seems to have foreshadowed my joining the Navy:

*A TOAST TO OUR NAVY*

*Here's to our Navy, their powerful might,*
*Our strength and our guardsmen through both day and night*
*Reckless and daring, more so than the rest,*
*The Navy is ours, and what's ours is the best.*

*First there's the Admiral, the serious one,*
*Who shows all the men how the work is to be done.*
*His ship is his castle; the sea is his home,*
*He's never content unless he's on foam.*

*Next there's the Officer, rigged out in glamour,*
*Gallant and carefree, he'll make your heart stammer.*
*A man at his best, no one can deny,*
*When his country's in danger, he's there standing by.*

*Then there's the Sailor, with airs of romance,*
*He loves to be happy, to sing and to dance.*
*He's all out for fun when he is on the shore*
*And yet he's the bravest in time of a war.*

*Brave men man our ships in this fight of today,*
*They're strong and courageous and yet always gay.*
*Good luck to these heroes, the young and the old,*
*God bless them and guard them, the Blue and the Gold!*

# The Wavey Navy Story

The WAACs (Women's Army Auxiliary Corps) were already part of the Army. Female Navy officers had been in training since July 1942. They were really the first to break into this man's world, setting up protocol, getting uniforms designed – even naming the new arm of the Navy. How they managed to accomplish all they did in such a short time is astonishing.

I drove the Navy recruiters crazy while waiting to hear when they were taking females. Finally, in August of 1942, word came – the Navy was enlisting women! As soon as I possibly could, I was in Philadelphia filling out papers and taking the necessary tests.

At that time, I pictured WAVES stationed near home doing office work, just as the yeomanettes had been during World War I. I knew that many of them had worked in Philadelphia, which had a large Navy shipyard and many government offices. That would certainly work for me. Armed with my office work experience and my enthusiasm to join the military, I passed all the tests along with 91 other girls from the Philadelphia area.

The next step was the physical exam. The physical consisted of wrapping yourself in a sheet and going from room to room for different examinations. The breast and heart exam room was unbelievable.

Keep in mind we were the first women to go through this in the Navy. When I got to one of the rooms, I truly thought I'd made a mistake. I opened the door and it looked as if a big conference was in progress. It was full of officers sitting around a long table. The room was blue with cigar and cigarette smoke. I was assured that I was in the right room, so up on a table, down with the sheet, and on with the exam. Was I that naïve to believe that it took that many doctors to agree that my heart and breasts were suitable for service? It seemed a little unusual, but authority intimidated me. After all, the Navy could do no wrong!

The interview regarding which training school we would attend came next. Our choices at that time were yeoman (office work), storekeeper (in charge of supplies), or radio operator. I knew nothing about radio, but was well qualified for yeoman. The sailor doing the interview, however, felt that RCA was an excellent background for radio. Thus, I opted for the radio school.

During that same interview, the location of the school I would attend was determined. Training schools were located in Oklahoma, Indiana, and Wisconsin. The sailor suggested that Madison, Wisconsin, the location for

# WAVE!

Miss Helen Edgar (8-10 Engineering 631) first girl from Special Apparatus Engineering to join the WAVES. She is going in as an apprentice radio operator, reporting to University of Wisconsin for training, October 8. The girls in the department gave her a send-off party at Neil Deighan's on Saturday, September 26. good luck, Helen!

A notice of my enlistment that appeared in the RCA newsletter.

WHY SHOULD WE NOT BE HOME AND GRIEVING
SINCE HELEN WILL SOON BE LEAVING?
INSTEAD WE SIT AROUND AND GRIN
OR WEEP LARGE TEARS INTO OUR GIN.

NO MORE WE'LL SEE HER SUNNY SMILE
OR HEAR HER OWN PECULIAR STYLE
OF SPEECH, OR SHARE THE GENTLE DIS-
POSITION OF THIS CARE-FREE MISS.

SHE DIDN'T SAY A SINGLE WORD.
A PATRIOTIC CALL SHE HEARD—
NOW, SOON SHE WILL REPORT FOR DUTY,
AND SHE'LL BECOME A "WAVE"ING BEAUTY.

Part of a nice goodbye card, signed by all my co-workers at RCA.

radio training, sounded the most interesting, so Wisconsin it was.

We had the formal swearing-in as a group. My heart was beating hard and my hands were cold and damp. We raised our right hands for the big commitment to live and/or die for our country. I recall the solemn, serious atmosphere in that room. There we were, young women swearing their complete loyalty to the Navy and our country. I'm sure none of us had the remotest idea of what we were in for, but we were willing.

On October 9th, 1942, 91 young girls from the Philadelphia area gathered at Penn Station to depart for their training schools. Twelve of the group were from south Jersey. My school friends, work comrades, family, and current love Wally were all there to say goodbye. The days immediately preceding our departure were filled with many parties and lots of publicity. Local papers and the RCA newsletter did articles and took pictures. It was a kind of glamour and attention I wasn't accustomed to, but I enjoyed it to the fullest. We boarded the train and headed into the unknown – scared, excited, and full of pride.

## A New Life

Up to this point I'd never been west of Pennsylvania, north of New York, or south of Delaware. It was unheard of in those days for girls to leave home. I had expected duty near home, and here I was on my way to Madison, Wisconsin. I had no idea what to expect.

Upon arrival, we discovered we'd be living on the University of Wisconsin campus. The university had contracted with the Navy to house, feed, and allow the use of their facilities to train Navy personnel. There were 480 WAVES on board.

I was assigned to Barnard Hall, a woman's dormitory. The building was four stories tall, traditional and elegant with rich, warm woods, a grand entrance and large foyer. The bottom level held the dining room, kitchen, recreation room, a library, and offices. An imposing wooden staircase led from the foyer to the upstairs where the bedrooms and bathrooms were located. Our bedroom had a bunk bed and a window seat that overlooked the campus, lush with trees and lawn.

It was a lovely place to be, especially in the month of October. Leaves were turning colors, giving a rainbow of oranges, yellows, reds, rust, and all shades of brown. We were surrounded by beauty.

This was a special time for me, because I could get a small taste of what it felt like to be in college. My schooling had been high school, followed by shorthand and typing courses in business school. I always had the feeling of being "less than," both intellectually and socially. There hadn't been enough money for both my brother and me to attend college.

Navy men were also in training on campus, but we didn't see much of them other than when marching between classes. During free time and on weekends, there was some socializing, but not much. We were closely chaperoned. We did have some dances and teas that the Navy men attended, along with some soldiers, but these were few and far between.

The local people were marvelous and so friendly. They made every effort to welcome us and make us feel at home. We had many invitations to Sunday family dinners. Our uniforms hadn't been designed yet, let alone issued, so our only identification was the horrible black oxfords we were required to wear. In town, everyone looked at our feet first to identify us.

I was fortunate to meet, through a mutual friend from RCA, a family who took me in and entertained me during my free time. They introduced me to a nice boy, John, and whenever I went an outing with them, John came along as my date.

Nice boy is a perfect description of John. He was of medium height and build, wore glasses, and was average looking. It was comfortable to be with him. John later joined the Army and suffered terrible frostbite in the Battle of the Bulge. I did hear years later that he married and had a family.

We had great times. We enjoyed Madison to its fullest, going to football games and rallies, rides in the country past farms and lakes, and, of course, family dinners.

When I graduated from training, John sent me long-stemmed red roses that I put on our window seat in our room. Unfortunately, the window was cracked open for air and they were dead as doornails and black by morning. It was February in Wisconsin – a little nippy.

Our months of training were rough on us pampered civilians. We rose before dawn, showered and cleaned our rooms, all before breakfast. Then it was out to muster, marching in platoons to and from classes. It was rigorous, but exhilarating and lots of fun. We sang songs as we marched and really bonded.

—     —     —

One of the songs we sang was "Here Come the WAVES" to the tune of "Anchors Aweigh":

*"Here Come the WAVES"*

*Dressed in our Navy blues, Here come the WAVES,*
*Each heart is Navy true, We're loyal all the way.*
*No job's too great a task; we're here to serve.*
*Each lass is proud to be a member of the USN Reserve.*

*Heave ho! There sailor, Everybody Hup-to while you may.*
*Heave ho! There sailor, Everybody up at break of day.*
*Roll along, sing a song,*
*though you're up at break of day, HEY!*

*We'll help you win this war; we'll do our share,*
*Backing our Navy boys on land, at sea and in the air.*
*Our course is chartered now; we'll never swerve,*
*We're very proud to be the Women of the USN Reserve.*

We also sang *"It's a Grand Old Flag"* and *"Here Comes the Navy"* to the tune of *"The Beer Barrel Polka."* It was quite a sight to see and hear all the squads of WAVES and sailors marching and singing, up hill and down dale, all over the campus.

The WAVES attracted girls from all parts of the country and all walks of life - Edith Gould from the financial family and Emily Saltonstall, daughter of Senator Saltonstall, among them. There we all were, trying to learn how, as females, to be sailors and radiomen.

We studied the Blue Jacket manual and learned the meaning of words like chow, head, taps, and reveille. I remember the futility of their trying to teach us to tie knots. They eventually gave up on that one.

We were taught rules and regulations. The old chief had us convinced that we'd be shot at dawn or hung on the yardarm if we broke any rules. My understanding of the yardarm was that in the old Navy days they hung sailors on it for treason.

Another requirement was to learn Morse code. We sat at long counter top desks with typewriters and headphones. It got so that we heard code everywhere - even the steam radiators in our rooms seemed to be sending code! I must say, we did learn it.

We also had to adjust to typing on the teletype. My experience at RCA was a big help with this, although the regular beat and light touch on the

*I am on extreme left*

University WAVES learn billiards from expert Peterson

We learned all kinds of important stuff.

Some cold-looking WAVES tramping through the snow.

keyboard was different from the old trusty Underwood typewriter. I had become a consistently error-free typist while working at RCA because I had to make eight copies with carbon paper. One tends to improve after having to erase eight pages after each error!

I bluffed my way through the classes on radio itself and how it works. I didn't understand it then and still don't. Another class was Communication Procedures. This was mostly memorizing and getting familiar with message set-up, Navy code words, and codes of Navy bases.

The Navy loves inspections! In our barracks they used white gloves looking for dust. We had to make up the bunks with tight sheets and hospital-style corners. Everything had to be neat, neat, neat. We had inspections for uniforms, shiny shoes, and lockers. Anything that stood still was fair game.

One inspection that stands out in my memory took place when we first arrived at Madison. About fifty of us were put in a room and told by a corpsman (a young sailor in medicine) to strip to the waist. This had become an ordinary procedure for us, so we did. In came a retinue of "brass" - doctors, corpsmen, and nurses.

They stopped dead in their tracks and asked us what in the world was going on? After we explained that we had been told to strip, the head doctor yelled, *"For an athlete's foot inspection?"*

—         —         —

We did a lot of drilling and marching; in squads, we marched to and from classes. We used the football field for training. Learning to march in formation took discipline and was totally alien for most of us. I had some experience from my Drum and Bugle Corps days, but the Navy was much stricter.

We took turns doing night patrol duty in two-hour stints, which required walking the halls and then resting in between on hard benches in a cage located in the main lobby. It was hard to stay awake and then get up for the grueling routine the next day.

My roommate, Sissie, was from Maine. She was quite a character. We often studied after lights-out in our bunk with flashlights under the blankets - a necessary method to keep from getting caught (the roaming patrols listened for noise and looked for light under our doors). I remember once we were memorizing "The Star Spangled Banner," which I already knew, but by the time I got through helping Sissie, neither of us could remember all the words.

Sissie's personality and physical appearance matched my mental picture of people from New England. She was strong, rugged, and straight as an

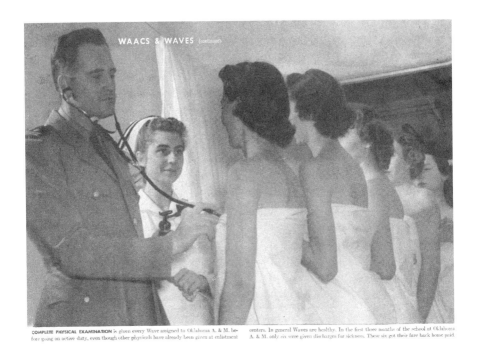

COMPLETE PHYSICAL EXAMINATION is given every Wave assigned to Oklahoma A. & M. before going on active duty, even though other physicals have already been given at enlistment. centers. In general Waves are healthy. In the first three months of the school at Oklahoma A. & M. only six were given discharges for sickness. These six got their fare back home paid.

Are they kidding?  Nothing like my physical !

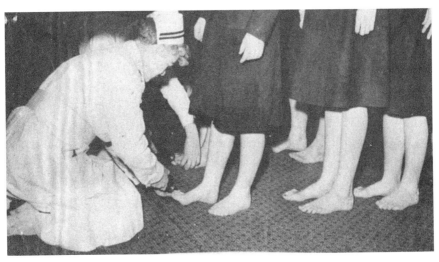

A typical athlete's foot inspection.  Given the female nurse, shirts most likely on!

arrow. Even her facial features were sharp and definite. You just knew she could rise at dawn, milk the cows, gather the eggs, and then cook breakfast. She had a delicious sense of humor and was lots of fun.

We enjoyed great food in our dining room. Large, round wooden tables gave us a perfect place and time to be with our new friends and get better acquainted. We always had a lot to share, because we were from such diversified backgrounds and experiences. One girl ate her food European style, meaning she held her fork in the left hand and used her knife to pile it with food. We had certainly never seen that before. Being the yokels that we were, we just assumed she had bad table manners.

Several memories that stand out: Going to the corner drug store after class for the best hot chocolate and Thomas' English Muffins dripping with butter and jam. Football games on Saturday afternoon. Marching and walking on crunchy leaves in the fall, snow in the winter. Ice cold rooms at night, being in wonderful shape from our rigorous routine. Comradeship and fun, exhaustion and good sleep. Learning to share. Previously, I'd always had my own room and my own things. Now it was '"ours," not "mine."

The first Christmas was a disaster. Every time Bing Crosby's *"White Christmas"* came on the radio, the tears flowed. We were one homesick group of sailors! I really felt that if we weren't so terrified of the "shot at dawn" thing or the dreaded yardarm, we'd all have gone AWOL (absent without leave).

It was around this time that I got a pass and went to Chicago to meet my brother on a Sunday. Somehow, Jim managed to convince a photographer to open his studio and take our picture for Mom and Dad. That's about all we had time for since each of us had to catch a train back to our respective bases. It was good to see him, and he looked fantastic in his uniform.

## Uniforms

Our uniforms came through around the end of November. They were well worth waiting for, designed by Mainbocher. We truly did like them, and I can't explain how very proud and elegant they made us feel. To don either the dress blues or summer whites to go on duty or into town was a pleasure. The total look affected our posture and even the way we walked.

The wool fabric was of wonderful quality that would last for years. We wore a white shirt with black tie tied in the traditional Navy square knot.

At Barnard Hall, before uniforms.

Finally, we got our uniforms!

Even the army joined the celebration. Theda Anderson of West Virginia has Pvt. William Arterburn of Tennessee as an escort at a dance in the Union Hall

My friend Theda.

My brother Jim and I, Chicago, 1942.

Our radio emblem and rank were worn on the upper left arm. Our hats were of soft fabric with a small brim. Black shoes were a must. At first we wore oxfords, but eventually pumps were permitted. (This was much later.)

Our summer whites were the same style as our dress blues. They were gabardine and were worn with white shoes. We were also issued gray-and-white striped seersucker dresses for summer and coveralls for hanging out.

Later, we figured out ways to make our uniforms even more attractive. We ironed pleats in the gores of our skirts and put a little starch in our summer seersucker dresses. We also got away with wearing the officers' long-sleeved white silk shirts.

Because we had to wear uniforms at all times, we wore exotic underwear. We were gorgeous undressed, long before Victoria's Secret. This was our way of making ourselves feel more feminine.

## Anchors Aweigh

We graduated from training the first week of February 1943. I missed the graduation ceremony, though. I was in sick bay, running a slightly high temperature. As a precaution, the doctors wouldn't release me, which was frustrating to say the least. I had, however, passed the course, and I received my diploma and rejoined my group in time for our departure.

No one knew where we were going - we were only told we'd be going to a Navy base somewhere in the United States. Farewells were difficult - we'd become very close.

We left Madison in groups under sealed orders. Our train was full of soldiers at either end, with us closed off in the middle. The trains were old, brought out of the train graveyard, I'm sure. They even smelled old. The stiff hard seats were covered in dark green plush fabric.

After leaving St. Louis, our officer in charge opened the "top secret" orders. We learned we were on our way to Corpus Christi, Texas. This was the end of the world as we knew it. We had five days to report for duty.

—  —  —

Several other girls and I got off the train at the next stop and headed home. We crossed the tracks and caught the next train coming through. This time the trains were packed with soldiers, sailors, and civilians. In these close quarters, you had to be friendly. It was nothing to fall asleep on someone's shoulder or lap.

# NEW YORKER

Boy, were the trains crowded during the war!

I ended up having about twenty-four hours in Collingswood before I had to get back on the train to Texas. A really short stay at home, but well worth the trip. At that time we had no idea when we'd be able to return, either for a trip or to stay. I felt I just had to touch base with the family.

## Corpus Christi

Corpus Christi Naval Air Station is a large base located on the Gulf of Mexico. It was then a relatively new base, having opened in March of 1941. It consisted of rows and rows of barracks, administration buildings, a movie theater, swimming pools, officers' housing, and a ship's store where we purchased our personal items, such as laundry soap, toothpaste, cigarettes, candy, and snacks. We also had a Post Office, a library, and a chapel. It was a self-contained city.

There was an airport, of course, with hangars that housed a large variety of aircraft for advanced training, transport, and utility runs (such as mail delivery to the auxiliary bases). Pensacola (Florida) and Corpus were the two main bases used for the final phase of Naval aviator training. Pilots graduated and received their wings at these bases

All construction on the base was of wood siding, painted gray with white trim. We had buses that ran frequently with designated stops for long trips across the base or into town. These buses also went to outlying installations - smaller bases under the jurisdiction of the main base.

—      —      —

On arrival in Corpus, I was assigned to a barracks located at the rear of the base. The building contained enough room for seventy-eight of us on each side of our barracks, with double bunks arranged in groups of four and lockers in between. I had an upper bunk located by the back door, giving me privacy and fresh air. All the girls on our side of the barracks were from Madison and were radio operators. The other wing housed the yeomen.

—      —      —

I met Theda when we both got off the train en route to Corpus and went home for the few days. We became close friends and remained so for many years. She was from Shinnston, West Virginia, and looked like actress Susan Hayward. Her mother had named her after Theda Bara, a movie star from the silent film era.

With brother Jim on leave back home.     Shopping & Doughnuts with Janet.

Base Swimming Pool.

Theda, with long, thick, reddish-brown hair, white alabaster skin, and blue eyes, was a warm cuddly type, and had a smile that melted all in her presence. She was feminine to the core, with a southern accent that added to her charm. Theda seemed innocent - however, looks were very deceiving. She was able to con and manipulate at will, and had no guilt about her actions.

— — —

When we checked in, we were automatically put on restriction for thirty-six hours. Theda talked me into going to a movie on base on our first day there. During the movie, I kept telling Theda that we should go back to the barracks, but her reply was, *"Oh, they won't care if we're a little late. We can stay 'til the end of the picture."*

We didn't get back to barracks until fifteen minutes after curfew. The female ensign on duty put us on report and took our passes and identification tags. There we were, our first day on base, and in trouble already.

When we reported to the radio shack in the Communications building the next day, we tried to hide at the back of the group. Monty, a salty old Navy chief, spotted me. He called me up front and asked for my identification, which, of course, I did not have. He couldn't believe I was in trouble already.

In the Navy, it is tradition to use last names. Monty nicknamed me "Eager" right on the spot, since my last name was Edgar, and he said I was eager for the wrong stuff. At that time there was a movie called *Johnny Eager*. Theda never liked the *"Eager"* label so I ended up being called Johnny. Monty had also caught Theda without her identification. He marveled at our ability to get on report so quickly before we'd even checked in for duty.

— — —

Located behind our barracks were long wooden slatted tables, used as drying racks for laundry. Being clever and needy, we learned to use them for tanning beds. In the summer in Corpus it got too hot to stay out there very long, but when the weather was nice, it became a great place to hang out and talk girl talk.

Tanning and looking good without stockings (and who wanted to wear them in that Texas heat?) was a top priority. A lot of us resorted to using cosmetic tanning lotion to tan our legs. It seemed to work but presented a problem we never solved. The gunk rubbed off on anything it touched and didn't go well on our dates' dress whites or navy blues. I'm sure by now they've improved these artificial tanning products, but I never tried them

Mom visiting me in Texas.

Sunny and I on drying racks.

Outside the U.S.O. Club.

again because of the disasters we'd had.

Any repair work in the barracks was done by crews under supervision. The warning call to us was *"Man on board!"* What tickled me was observing that any female caught naked would automatically cover her breasts and let the rest hang out.

Our barracks were guarded at all times – usually by men so old they could hardly have done anything if challenged. No doubt that was on purpose. They didn't want foxes guarding the hens.

We ate in a chow hall shared with the Navy chiefs, so we had great food. The Navy is good to its chiefs. We carried tin trays, went through the chow line, and sat at long tables together. The procedure was to put the main course on one side of tray, eat that, and then spin the tray around to finish dessert. Our eating time was limited, as we were fed in shifts. We'd catch it if we didn't finish the food, no matter what it was – tough meat, cold eggs – we were supposed to eat it all. After we finished, we took our tray to a garbage can, scraped it clean, and placed it in a stack.

After our first year, the chief in charge of the chow hall put us on a diet. He said we were all gaining too much weight, particularly in the rear end. After that, there were more salads and fewer sweets, but we still had baked beans for breakfast every Saturday morning.

The chow hall sailors were good to us. When we came back to base late at night after partying in town, the cooks invited us in and fed us steak and eggs. We usually needed it.

We had loudspeakers in the barracks for "Taps" and "Reveille" and any announcements. The sailors loved it when they could announce at Taps *"Okay, girls, man your bunks."* It was a daily joke.

Our radio shack was located on the top floor of the Administration Building, on the other side of the base from our barracks. Walking from our barracks to the radio shack was invigorating and pleasant. The Texas skies were so blue, with wonderful white puffy clouds. Sunrise and sunset were indeed treats for our senses, with myriad pinks, purples, oranges, blues, and greens. I had never seen anything like it in New Jersey. The open spaces were awesome and life was good.

One of the most thrilling moments for me was the flag ceremony every morning. It was our duty to signal the start of the raising of the flag from our radio room overlooking the compound. The station Marine Corps Band and the military color guard marched in formation to the compound adjacent to the flagpole.

Administration Building.

A flight of SNJs. I had my first plane ride in an SNJ, and years later my husband Chuck and I owned one.

Typical base humor.

We waited at the window near the clock, called out *"Stand By!"* and then, right on the minute, *"Colors!"* The station band played *"The Star Spangled Banner"* as the Marine Honor Guard hoisted the flag up the pole. The whole base would stop, face the location of the flag, and salute. It was one majestic moment. It made me proud to be an American. I especially liked it when I was the one who shouted colors. It felt as if I was personally starting up the whole world.

The Communications office was a large, open room with banks of teletype machines, counter desks with earphones, and hand keys or "bugs" for transmitting Morse code. The bugs were used by those with more experience who could send code faster. We could do about twenty words per minute on the hand key. The more seasoned radiomen could do at least forty or fifty words per minute with their bug. They were *good*.

We had microphones and receivers for voice communication and a Western Union counter in one corner. A civilian worked the Western Union counter from 8 a.m. until midnight. We watched over the teletype and telephone during the mid-watch. It was a noisy and friendly work atmosphere.

We worked in eight-hour shifts, nine days in a row. During the nine days we had duty, we stayed on base most of the time. We really had to. We were too tired to do much else.

$-$     $-$     $-$

The first three days we worked from 0800 to 1600 (8 a.m. to 4 p.m.), the next three days from 1600 to midnight, and the last three days from midnight to 0800. (That was the rough one; you never got used to it.) Then we had three days' liberty.

The Officer of the Day and other communications officers were located upstairs from the radio shack. Our closest contacts were the chief and supervisors. The supervisor, usually a Radioman 1st Class, was on each watch. He designated our duties and oversaw the work activity. The chief was on deck for the day watch.

When on duty from 0800 to 1600, our energy level was good. We got up at 0600, showered, had breakfast in the chow hall, and then walked across the base to the Administration Building. This was a fifteen-minute walk past the enlisted men's barracks, the swimming pool, and other buildings on base. At first, there was a lot of cat-calling and whistling, but that tapered off. As time went by, more and more WAVES came on base. We ceased being unusual, and became a normal part of the military community.

Our favorite watch was the 1600 to midnight shift. We could sleep in, go for breakfast later, do laundry or other errands, and report in at four in the afternoon. It was still quite busy on that watch, and that helped pass the time. Not as many officers (we called them "brass") were around, so it was a more relaxed atmosphere. Sometimes, we'd take the station bus to town at midnight for a shrimp cocktail, then head back to base and bed. It was about a half-hour ride each way, but it was worth it.

The midnight to 0800 shift was a killer. We called it the mids, or the midwatch. Our body clocks never adjusted. At about 0500 our energy sagged and time stretched long because there was little to do. Once off-duty, we had breakfast and went to the barracks to crash.

## Gaining Acceptance

This was a scary time for us. We were working side by side with seasoned Navy men and we were well aware of the negative feelings about us. We'd heard all about our joining the Navy to "service" the men. We ignored this and showed them we could and would be a valuable asset.

At first, there was tension between the men and their new female co-workers. Radio operators were a close-knit group. We knew they didn't believe we could do that kind of work. No way! We were more or less ignored. The attitudes of some of the men bordered on hostility toward us. The military was a man's world and we were invading it!

An example of this attitude was the following that appeared in a local newspaper:

*The WAVES and WAACs are leaving,*
*And the WAAFs are beginning to go,*
*And I know that the Lord with his infinite ken*
*Has surely been planning it so.*

*If they only will go where there is no print —*
*Where static controls the air*
*Where the wires are cut and the poles are down*
*Where it is strictly their own affair*

*While we fight it out in our masculine style*
*In peace and in social bliss*

*Without having to stop while cocking the cannon*
*To give the poor floozies a kiss.*

*With the end of the war, we'll send Eleanor*
*To bring the poor darlings to light,*
*And then meet their ship in the deep of the drink*
*And torpedo the damn thing on sight.*

We knew we had to be quick studies, do the work as well as we could, and not react to verbal slurs. As the Navy men often said, *"Stay on course."* This was difficult because we'd gone into the service with such enthusiasm, and now felt unwanted.

## Prejudice

As a child growing up in Philadelphia, and later New Jersey, I was exposed to racial and religious prejudice. The common belief was that if you weren't white, middle-class, and Protestant, you were not to be trusted.

One of my early recollections is of going to a Chinese restaurant for take-out and being protected by the adults as though I might be in danger. The man at the counter gave me some lichee nuts. I couldn't understand their attitude when he was being so kind.

During the election between Al Smith and Herbert Hoover, it was down-right dangerous to be on the streets. Al Smith was a Catholic, and in those days the idea of a Catholic President was unheard of. The tension between Catholics and Protestants was alarming.

—    —    —

I had a Catholic playmate, Gerry, who took me along with her to confession and mass. When Dad's mother heard about this sinful activity, she insisted that my mother forbid me to enter a Catholic church. She was raised an Orange Protestant in Northern Ireland .

My other grandmother, nee Murphy, had left the Catholic Church. Rumors were that something about the priests having been involved with the nuns had caused her to leave. Who knows?

Only one black family lived in Collingswood. They ran a small shoe repair shop on the main street. We never saw them around town. They stayed completely to themselves.

In addition to the attitude directed at women that I experienced, I observed other forms of racism and prejudice on base. For example, the gates on the base were manned by young Marines. This duty was the only authority they had, and in my opinion, they misused it at times. The enlisted men returning from town were given the inevitable "short arm" inspection. This was a check for venereal disease. Since alcohol was not allowed on base, they were also searched for hidden bottles. The treatment of the black men was drastically different. It was much more severe - they were man-handled and talked to disrespectfully.

—    —    —

Another incident that shocked me involved the crew I worked with in the radio shack. Early on, we went to a restaurant for dinner. Our waiter was black. Theda and I chatted with him about choices on the menu and thanked him for his help. When he left our table, a supervisor we worked with gave us Holy Hell. He let us know in no uncertain terms that when he was present, we were not to socialize or even be friendly with a black person (not the term he used). Theda and I were speechless, but we quickly got the picture of how he felt about race.

## Duty

The enlisted men and chiefs we worked with were most supportive once they realized that we meant business and were there to work. We had some likable first-class radiomen who helped us with the work and taught us what we needed to know. Occasionally, they laced our coffee with booze on the mids to keep us going.

When we went to the chow hall for breakfast, we brought back goodies for the married enlisted men. They lived in Navy housing on the base, so they didn't eat in the chow hall. One supervisor, Horne (last name), loved baked bean sandwiches. Every Saturday when baked beans were on the menu, we brought him sandwiches.

Horne tried to convince us that he was bald on the front of his head because of his wife's pushing and pulling on his hair in ecstasy. He and his wife Polly entertained us frequently. Polly introduced me to my first taste of avocado in salad.

Rudy, a big, strapping first-class radioman, was a teddy bear, but he had a serious problem with alcohol. We were forever taking turns driving to town to rescue him from a bar and/or a brawl.

The Navy shore patrol knew him and often called us so they wouldn't have to put him in the brig (jail). He also had a bad habit of smoking in bed. This necessitated multiple mattresses being tossed out of the bedroom window, on fire from a lit cigarette. To know him was to love him, so we all protected and rescued him when necessary, and that was frequently.

One night we were having our usual discussion about the pros and cons of women in the service. One old Texan just sat back and listened. After a while, he finally spoke up, saying, *"I don't know whether it's good or bad to have women in the service, but one thing I do know. It sure smells better around here!"*

Most of the time it was a comfortable, stress-free environment, but when the commander came on the scene, we all had to straighten up and mind our manners. His office was upstairs near the code room so we didn't see much of him. We were grateful for that!

—        —        —

Our work consisted of teletype and copying code from a "Fox" schedule that was sent continuously to all military bases twenty-four hours a day. It was a constant flow of information transmitted to all Navy stations and ships at sea. It was more or less a CNN radio station of the Navy.

We received information on all activity and the general status of all military operations. It was grueling duty. We took turns on it and were relieved every hour to do other things.

The teletype machines carried the heaviest load of communication. To work on these, we either typed directly on-line or cut tape and fed it into a small attachment and when clear, we could activate and send it. The direct typing required a steady, perfect touch at 40 words per minute. It was the easiest to do when the message was short. For longer transmissions, cutting tape was more practical.

We sent and received messages of all kinds. Some messages concerned mechanical difficulties and instructions regarding maintenance procedures. Routine information was in English. The secret and top secret messages were encoded. We took those upstairs to a separate office to be decoded.

There were different frequencies for each specialized type of transmission and facility. We had six auxiliary fields around Corpus: Kingsville, Rodd, Cabiniss, Cuddihy, Chase, and Waldron. We handled all administrative communications between our station and these outlying bases.

Naturally, we had contact with other Navy bases - Pensacola more than others, because it was also a flight training base. We had a lot of traffic from Washington, D.C., as well.

The workload varied, but we usually had enough activity to keep us going. We filed and ran messages upstairs to the code room and to other offices on the base. Messenger duty was welcomed. It got us out of the office for some fresh air and different scenery. We used a little Navy pickup truck to drive around the base.

We did a lot of joking around, chatting and coffee drinking. I don't think the coffee pot had ever been properly cleaned. The coffee could sure get your attention! At least it kept us awake. The conversations consisted of war stories, news about how things were going, and how we all wished it was over so that we could go home.

One sailor from Texas brought his guitar to work and serenaded us with cowboy songs on the mid-watch. My favorite was his rendition of *"The Yellow Rose of Texas."*

—    —    —

With such a cross-section of personalities and backgrounds, it was interesting to get to know each other and share our histories. The amazing part was how we all adapted and became soulmates. There was a strong feeling of unity. We worked, played, slept, and ate together. We even wore the same clothes. Of course, there were some differences and jealousies. Living under these circumstances, however, they usually got resolved fairly quickly.

WAVES couldn't be sent overseas or on board ship, but the Navy did open up Hawaii to us. We heard rumors about how strict they were in Hawaii, so we didn't ask to be transferred. We had it too good in Corpus, so why take a chance? We didn't know a thing about Hawaii except that Pearl Harbor was located there. We figured all they had to eat were pineapple and papaya.

One subject that tickled me was the brothels in Honolulu. Many men who served over there talked about Hotel Street with its myriad brothels. They told of the long lines of men waiting to get in, but, somehow, none of them had ever stood in those lines! I wonder who did?

We had periodic "Field Days," cleaning and mopping the radio shack. We would disappear into the head (ladies' room) and not come out until it was over, which drove Monty over the edge.

Monty was our chief and a delightful character. He was old-time Navy with hash-marks up his sleeve indicating length of service; one for every four-year stint. He was small of stature, with red curly hair and twinkling blue eyes. He was a delightful person, loving and caring. Most of the time we could sweet-talk Monty to get days off to accommodate our "date of the month."

He loved to tease and give us a hard time. He'd come into the radio shack, look around – hands on hips – and shake his head. He would then proceed to tell us how much money he could make if we'd quit *"giving it away"* in town, and let him handle us.

In the beginning, we had to participate in parades, drills, and uniform inspections. Monty would come by and whisper *"Stick out your chest, Eager."* Anything to get us giggling. Somehow or other, Monty got us excused from the parade drills and cleaning the barracks. Perhaps this was because he noticed we didn't do that stuff too well. That was keen, since we hated those duties. He used the angle that we should be exceptions because we worked around-the-clock shifts. After that, the "boots," or new WAVES on base, cleaned the barracks for us.

## Home Away from Home

The barracks consisted of two wings, joined in the middle by the recreation room, the head (bathroom), and the laundry room equipped with washing machines and ironing boards.

The office and bedroom of the WAVE in charge of the whole deal was located up front by our sleeping quarters. Ma Smith was our "Master at Arms." She was very intimidating, but that was her job. She was there to see that we didn't break any rules and that we kept our barracks neat and clean. She yelled at us for infractions like unmade beds, but underneath it all she was a sweetheart.

During our time-off periods, we usually stayed on base and, other than for short trips to the Post Office or Ship's Service Store, we were in the barracks. There was plenty to do to keep us busy. We had to do our laundry and make up the bunks with clean linen. It was a challenge for us to stow all of our uniforms, lingerie, and cosmetic necessities in our lockers and keep them neat for inspections. We all borrowed things from each other, and privacy was a thing of the past. Our universal agreement was that what is mine is yours and what is yours is mine. It worked.

In the summer months, we were into laundry, showers, and hair washing more than ever. Corpus was hot and humid, to say the least. Our uniform of the day when just hanging out was a towel wrapped around the body to stay as cool as possible.

The showers consisted of one big room with shower heads coming out of the walls. This didn't give us much privacy, but it was very friendly. Later, private stalls were put in for us, but to tell the truth, it was lonely. We'd become accustomed to our communal showers. After months of scrubbing and chatting together, it had become a great meeting place. So we just continued to use the old shower room.

—    —    —

If we'd held a boob contest, one of the girls, Margie, would have won it hands down. She was built like a brick outhouse and they were all real (there were no such thing as breast implants back then). I never did understand how they could stay up the way they did, being the size they were. She was about 5 feet 2 inches, with light brown hair, brown eyes, a narrow waist and those high, full, round breasts. She had no trouble getting dates.

There was an air of mystery about her that bewitched men. A rumor later had it that one of the cadets committed suicide when she dumped him. I do know the report was that his trainer plane just dived into the ground at full speed. We all hoped it was mechanical or something else that caused the crash, but we never did find out.

Several of the girls had good figures. One thing I noticed, though, was that even at our young age, there were very few of us who had really great breasts. That amazed me. There was the usual run of small pert boobs, large hanging boobs, the pancake type – a whole gamut of sizes and shapes. Enough on boobs. I'm getting worried about my sexual preference!

Sonja, a chic exotic WAVE of Russian descent, wore Shalimar perfume, and on her it smelled divine. I tried it, but it didn't work for me. I think it was designed for glamour girls, and Sonja indeed had glamour. She had a sexy European look, with long black hair pulled into a knot at the nape of her neck, olive skin, and dark eyes. I was a mongrel with light brown, naturally curly hair and hazel eyes. I settled for Ciara, a light, fresh scent.

—    —    —

Later, other barracks adjacent to ours housed mechanics, corpsmen, storekeepers, yeomen, and other classifications. To be honest, the radio operators were an isolated group. Because of our eight-hour, around-the-clock shift duties, we tended to live and socialize amongst ourselves. Our work hours and days off were varied. Our barracks were unique, with our coming and going at all hours. Ours was a more relaxed atmosphere – not as rigid and strict as others.

## Liberty

The usual routine at 0800 on the first day of liberty was to head directly for town. Corpus Christi was a typical Gulf town with fishing as one of the main industries and, of course, the Texas oil commercial enterprises.

It was a clean environment, built up from the waterfront with a few hotels, restaurants, and department stores. The base filled it with military personnel and a lot of activity. I'm sure it was good for the economy, but am not so sure that all the locals were pleased to have us there. We were, however, generally welcomed and made to feel at home.

We shopped in Corpus for luxuries such as make-up, toiletries, underwear, hosiery, and nightgowns. We ate Oysters Rockefeller, shrimp cocktails, scrambled eggs and chili (a Texas favorite) with cheese and onions. My introduction to Mexican food set up a life-long addiction that is still with me.

We had innumerable hotel room parties at the famous Driscoll Hotel. It was our favorite hotel, perhaps because of the legendary Clara Driscoll. It was said that she built it to spite the owner of another hotel, right next door. She didn't like the service at that establishment so she said she'd build one high enough to be able to spit on it. Rumor had it she'd wanted to do something worse than spit on it.

Clara Driscoll had quite an interesting life. She was born into a wealthy Texas family and married a famous newspaperman. She was named "Savior of the Alamo" because of a generous private donation. Her picture hung on the wall in the Capitol. She was our kind of girl – redheaded, vivacious, and fiery.

How can I possibly explain those days? We'd start at Shoop's, our favorite restaurant, then do some shopping, get a hotel room, and crash for a while. Our dates showed up later. Those darlings brought the brandy, creme de cocoa, and beer. We'd supply the whipping cream and ice. Brandy Alexanders go down easy. They taste like chocolate ice cream sodas, only better. They got us into a lot of trouble.

Parties just happened. By night time, we usually ended up with ten or twenty of us in one room. We drank rum and Cokes as well as beer, ate lots of food, and had great fun. Lots of music and whooping and hollering went on in our rooms. It became a heavy traffic area, with folks coming and going at all times of the night and day.

If one of us didn't have a date, it was not a problem. All one had to do was walk the halls or go to the dining room. Cadets or officers were available, ready and willing to join the festivities. There were so many cadets that we referred to them as our "hot and cold running cadets," on tap at any time.

—     —     —

It might sound as if we never dated enlisted men, but many girls did. I think it was rare for us to date sailors because most of the radio gang in our group were married and lived on base. We did have some office socials in town or at one of the supervisor's or chief's quarters on base.

We sat around talking and thinking up things to do and trouble we could get into. I will admit that when the drinking got heavy, there was a lot of passing out or taking naps. Any available space was used for sleeping, including the bathtub, closet, whatever. It got a little confusing what with all the bodies. It was hard to tell exactly what was going on and who was with whom. Besides, we really didn't care. At our age, and being at war, I don't think we were morally corrupt. Our hormones were at their peak. The present and the future were uncertain. Being intimate felt safe and secure. Sex was a way of being loved and it felt good.

When we would "settle down" and get serious with one of the cadets, of course we would rent a private room for our interludes. That was such a welcome respite. To have a few hours alone with the one you at that time thought you loved was Heaven. Contrary to popular belief, most of us went "steady" for several months and remained true to our current man. The main reason we changed to other dates was that the current man would graduate and leave for duty abroad. That lead to many hearthaches, but life went on and so did we.

Somehow our parties just seemed to grow and grow. One night a general or an officer of some rank came over, trying to get us to quiet down, threatening us with the Shore Patrol, hotel manager, anything. We invited him in and he stayed the rest of night. He was clothed in his military jacket to show his rank, with just his pajama bottoms underneath. We all were escaping the reality of why we were there and what was going on in the outside world. During our big parties, it was "no holds barred." I am prone to think there was more heavy petting than actual intercourse, but I'll admit I'm not sure.

Another pastime we loved was throwing water balloons out of the windows. It's a wonder we didn't kill someone. The hotel manager didn't like that activity. He often threatened us with eviction if we didn't stop.

During one party, one crazy guy stole the hotel elevator. He just kept pushing buttons and there was no catching him. That same nut stole the base bus once and got himself into a bit of trouble.

This particular cadet was dating one of our girls, Carrie. She was a serious type, pigeon-toed, and had big protruding eyes. She had a charming, fun personality. After her first date with this nut, she came back to base, sad and dejected. We asked her how it went and her reply was, *"Sex raised its ugly head."* None of us were surprised. She and Carl ended up married, and reared a family in California. He became a lawyer.

We did manage to go to the dining room at the hotel or some place in town when we got hungry. We spent the three days of our liberty driving on the beach, going to the USO, anything to be together and have fun. Our drinking and parties usually took place at night, but not every night. We couldn't keep up that pace. We had other things to do and places to go.

We met many celebrities. We saw Tyrone Power in town with a bevy of blondes, eating dinner at the Driscoll. He was having problems with Annabelle in those days, and we read his telegrams from her. They came in on our teletype from Western Union during the mid-watch. Good stuff.

Robert Taylor and Robert Stack came through town, too. We met Bob Stack at an apartment that some of the officers had. We had no clue at that time how big a star he would become. He was worried at the time that the war might hurt his career in films. Obviously, it didn't. He ended up his career on television with his *Unsolved Mysteries* show.

Downtown Corpus Christi is right on a bay and fronted with a stepped concrete sea wall. This was a great place to sit and watch the boats and birds. We went there frequently. At night we went there to enjoy the sea breezes and the peaceful, serene atmosphere. Texas skies are spectacular, morning, noon, and night. The stars really are big and bright, deep in the heart of that state.

One night while we were there, I had to go to the bathroom and decided to just go down to the bottom step to relieve myself. My friend Janet went with me, and our dates were told to turn their backs to us. It was dark and I didn't realize the tide had gone out. When I reached the bottom step, it was covered with slimy moss, and I went flying into the bay, taking Janet with me. All she wanted to know was whether I had "gone" yet. Of course I had, immediately upon hitting the warm water! We spent the next few hours trying to dry out our blues so we could go back to base. As I said, those uniforms could take anything, even a salt-water bath.

Being a female on a base with hundreds of men, it was easy to be popular - too easy. As I said, we dated lots of the cadets. After graduation, they got

# WAVE Radio Operators Here Year

### Seventy-One Girls Take Pride Being 'Firsts' On Station

**By ONE OF THE 71**

Do we recall . . .?

We do, with somewhat of a braggish air, that one year ago—31 January, dately speaking—the deck of the USS Corpus Christi quivered 'neath the footsteps of the first WAVE enlisted personnel.

The inner-thoughts of 71 radio-women would provide a priceless page for any Navy scrapbook. As no record was made of those first impressions, the best we can do is swap snatches of the highlights as we remember them:

**Endless Rows of Beds**

Barracks with endless rows of beds; tin cups which must be dunked; cups (two-fisted if you please) and without handles, and the futile task of consuming one-half grapefruit with a dainty implement, commonly known as a tablespoon.

But that was a year ago. We've come a long way since then, and know that we were probably the "bootiest of all boots!"

The WAVE family has grown by leaps and bounds until our throng of 71 is only a small part but we still take pride in being "firsts" and after all adjustments were made we decided we like it fine and hope you are the same.

**Here They Are**

Following are 65 of the WAVES here who comprised the original 71:

Grace J. Zinnik, Olive E. Barnes, Helen Baycar, Mary O. Baxter, Dorothy R. Shave, Dorothy E. Bellum, Eileen A. Blomquist, Lillian R. Bouvier, Florence E. Buckley, Aldeen B. Roberson, Helen J. Bush, Marcelle M. Lesire.

Eleanor J. Litwin, Loudella Lunn, Essie M. Parsons, Stella M. Mahler, Margaret J. McAtee, Idamae K. McClinton, Irene M. Lee, Sallie Miller, Margaret F. Molnar, Linda E. Niemeyer, Yolanda J. Hughes.

Marjorie S. Paterson, Mary E. Rutter, Felice J. Koibik, Beatrice C. Kobza, Helen J. E. Kirsch, Leola M. Kirk, Deborah Kirk, Margaret E. Ibbitson, Ruth V. Heisner, Dorothy C. Slusher, Olive R. Smith.

Janet K. Stucke, Mildred G. Taylor, Carolyn R. Throop, Audrey V. Weisiger, Joycelyn M. Carter, Helen M. Cassidy, Helen J. Caudle, Florence L. Daniels, Glee P. Davis, Agnes Evans, Mary I. Erdman, Lorraine L. White, Mary C. Freeman, Andree A. Goddard, Sophie M. Grohs, Virginia A. Luce, Theda F. Anderson.

Helen T. Edgan, Ethel E. Maloney, Vera E. Kapp, Braska S. Mann, Marjorie E. Court, Grace D. Niermeier, Leota M. Park, Elsie E. Rapoza, Lillian Rye, Anna 'dron, Sophie E. Wi:.ams, . Winters, Marion Gr.... ..zel Verdell.

With my old roommate Sissie on the Corpus Cristi seawall.

Shoops, our favorite restaurant.

Dinner with Mert the Marine, a real jokester.

their wings and away they flew. We didn't want to get too close to them. It became too painful, knowing they'd leave and we'd never see them again.

After about a year, the Navy went through the big purge. What we heard was that too many of the pilots were getting killed landing on carriers, in combat, and while flying. The powers-that-be decided that they were rushing them through training too fast, and not weeding out the ones who were incompetent. This was a sad time for the boys.

There were rumors about suicides. Being "washed out" of the program they loved was just too much for some of the cadets to deal with. Some transferred to other types of training – navigation, gunnery, and related fields. It was rough, but I think a necessary step to save lives.

## Shore Patrol

While in town on shore leave, we became well acquainted with the Navy police, known as the Shore Patrol. Unfortunately, these were times when we weren't on our best behavior.

–    –    –

My friend Theda had a serious problem with liberty. She was a rebel and prone to keep "civvies" (civilian clothes) in town and go out on her dates in them. The Shore Patrol had their eyes on her, and she was always getting caught and put on report. Her punishment was restriction to the barracks, with a big sign that said P.A.L. (Prisoner at Large) on her bunk. She ate lots and lots of Mars bars (her favorite), drank soda pop, spent many hours on the phone, and read racy romance magazines such as *True Story*.

The thing I loved about Theda was that nothing seemed to bother her. She just took things in her stride. So she got caught? Big deal. Maybe next time they wouldn't notice her. But they always did.

–    –    –

One of the girls, Bucky, started dating a Shore Patrol guy named Sam who rented a place off base. It was a great little house, built on a pier out in North Beach. He worked shifts similar to those of firemen, and when he had duty, he let us use his place.

We really enjoyed this respite from the routine of barracks and hotel rooms. It had a kitchen, but to be honest, not much in-depth cooking was done. We fixed a lot of hot dogs. The neighbors, who lived next door in an adjoining little house, were great to us and we hung out with them a lot.

At the house on Pier at North Shore, with neighbors and Sam, the friendly Shore Patrol guy who let us use it. I am on the right.

Dinner at the Swan Club, celebrating with our friends who had just gotten their wings. Left to Right: Ricky, Jane, Helen, and Paul.

We even managed to get invited occasionally to eat home-made spaghetti.

During the day we just kicked back and stayed in bathing suits all day, swimming and doing what we liked to do best – nothing. It was a welcome break. What I remember most about those sojourns is sleeping over the water out on the pier. It was like sleeping on a boat, with the smell of the sea and moonlight all around you. The bed would rock you to sleep. Peace and serenity.

—    —    —

Bucky broke off the relationship with Sam, and there went our beach House. Like everything else in life, we learned that change is inevitable.

## San Antonio

My boyfriend from home, Wally, kept in touch. In May of 1943, he arranged to come to San Antonio with his sister and her husband for a visit. I got liberty and took a bus to San Antonio to be with them for a few days.

That city was indeed a place of beauty, with the canal running through town, the spectacular Sunken Gardens, and so many trees and parks. Corpus was stark by comparison. San Antonio was mostly an Army town, and the enlisted men kept saluting me, as though I were an officer. They'd never seen the WAVE uniform, so I just saluted back. Why not? What I recall most about that trip is roasted rattlesnake meat in the park. We were told the usual - *"It tastes like chicken."* I'll never know. I just couldn't try it.

—    —    —

I'm not proud of this, but I had mixed feelings about Wally by this time. I felt a little embarrassed that he wasn't military. He had thyroid problems or some such thing that kept him out. I still really liked him, but not the way I had at home before the war when I was head over heels about him.

—    —    —

Wally gradually faded out of my life. We had no serious commitment - just an understanding that we were a couple and in love. After the war was over and I left home for good and relocated in California, the relationship ended. At this point he was a golf pro at one of our country clubs, back in New Jersey. He was looking good, but I guess that wasn't enough. He begged me to come back to New Jersey and marry him, but I had plans to head out. My lifestyle had changed drastically, and I needed to move on. He did marry, but I heard later that he'd died an alcoholic on skid row. What a sad ending.

## Fun and Games

Occasionally, we went to a waterfront hotel at North Beach. This was on the edge of Corpus, with a pier built out into the Gulf. It had a good beach and great swimming. Sometimes there were lots of jellyfish, but after we'd had a few beers, when it was hot and humid, we simply went in with them.

At one party, for cadets who were graduating, one poor soul got drunk and passed out on the beach. We finally turned him over when we noticed he was starting to look like a cooked lobster. He got so burned that he ended up in sick bay and missed graduation. It was against Navy rules to allow yourself to get that burned, and he was duly punished. Maybe hung on the good old yardarm, who knows?

During one big bash out at North Beach with our gang from the radio shack, things got a little wild. We staged a big mock wedding. One sailor I worked with had a crush on me, and we were the wedding couple. Mack was an attractive guy from Florida, very sincere, but relatively inexperienced in dealing with women. He was as cute as a button, and I really liked him as a friend. (God, those words can be cruel.)

He was of medium-size, had black curly hair, clear blue eyes, and looked fantastic in his bell-bottoms. How I loved those bell-bottoms! The sailors looked so sexy in them with their tight little butts. They had a devil-may-care attitude that captured my heart.

It seemed like fun at the time, but poor Mack wanted it to be real and was crushed after it was over and I told him "no go." Crazy times and crazy behavior.

–       –       –

Another spot for fun and getting away was Port Aransas on Mustang Island - a quiet fishing village back then. It was rumored that FDR had gone fishing there. We had to drive thirty miles out of Corpus Christi through small towns to connect with the ferry that took us out to the island. Upon arrival, we walked through the town and down to the beach. The town was small, with an old wooden hotel on the main street, one grocery store, and an assortment of beach cottages.

It was lovely there – wild horses, sand dunes covered with sea oats, white sand beaches, and emerald water. Beauty and tranquility beyond belief. We went way out in the Gulf to a sand bar, basked in the sun, and soaked in the warm salt water for hours.

It was necessary to keep an eye on the time, as the ferry stopped running at 1800. If we missed it, we'd be stranded. Whenever possible, we rented a beach cottage for two or three days. That was sheer luxury. We walked on the wet sand at the water's edge for miles. It was fun to romp around the sand dunes. At night we turned on the radio, played cards and talked.

—    —    —

We went down to Laredo a few times. It was a fun town, right on the Mexican border. We walked across a bridge to Nuevo Laredo to shop and of course to drink their tequila. We traveled by bus and rented a hotel room on the Texas side of town. Laredo was dirty and crowded – packed with military on leave.

On one of these trips we took a girl named Hilda with us. She was a strict, old-maid school teacher type. She was an average-looking female, with short brown hair and fair, pock-marked skin – one of those people who melt into the background. She'd never imbibed alcohol and was still a virgin.

Out of the goodness of our hearts, we introduced her to Brandy Alexanders, and then hooked her up with an Air Force officer. They ended up in our hotel room for the next two days and wouldn't let us in. We spent the night in the hotel lobby. Our friend was no longer a virgin, and from then on she was totally out of control. The remarkable thing to me was that she remained a quiet and reserved person, verifying the old saying that still waters run deep.

The Laredo incident was followed by Hilda's getting herself plastered and laid at every opportunity. At our parties at North Beach, she'd get loaded and disappear with a cadet or officer. During one party she passed out, fell off a pier, and had to be fished out of the Gulf. When we went to Port Aransas, she often stayed out in the sand dunes overnight. They had Navy Shore Patrol on duty on horseback, and we always suspected they were riding more than their horses when Hilda showed up.

When hurricanes hit, and they did, we were confined to base. During one storm, the radio gang hung out at Chief Monty's house. He headed for the commissary and the chow hall, gathering as much food as possible. We camped out there, sleeping, eating, playing cards, and waiting out the storm. We left the house only to go on watch until the hurricane was over.

Wives of military men seem to be blessed with the patience and flexibility to be perfect hostesses. His wife, Mary, was a saint to put up with us, though after a particularly wild night, she did complain about the long black scuff marks she was going to have to scrub. I remember her pointing them out to us, high on the wall next to a cot. We all knew they were from Hilda's shoes.

## Homosexuality

In those days, the gay world was unfamiliar to most of us. I remember when I became old enough to be aware of this other lifestyle. It was during my high school years, and our church organist was caught "playing" with some of the small boys' organs. That was a scandal that shocked the whole town. Growing up, I was completely in the dark on all these taboo subjects. I'd been raised with two men in the house, my father and brother, but had never seen a male naked. Sex was not discussed, at least not by our parents. I had to rely on information from an aunt and friends.

Once I was in the service, living in such close quarters with so many women, it was darn near impossible to avoid noticing things about some of their tendencies. We had some females who were really heavy-duty masculine types on base, mostly the aircraft mechanics and maintenance women.

We had a really cute radio operator named Julie in our barracks. She was part Indian and extremely attractive. She had a small but good figure, dark wavy hair, beautiful brown eyes, and a delightful personality. She had no problem attracting men. We heard that she was engaged to marry a handsome officer. This was no surprise to us.

We had a few yeomen and office workers in our barracks with us. One of them, Edna, a blond with short straight hair, had sort of an abrupt way about her, but she was friendly. She was somewhat masculine but not overly so. She was a quiet, private type, slight of build, the kind of person you really don't pay much attention to. Our first inkling that Edna and Julie were "different" was seeing them together in the chow hall and around the base. The next clue was seeing them go off to town on liberty together. Then we heard that Julie had broken off her engagement.

As time went on, it became extremely apparent that they had more than a casual friendship. They became closer and closer, spending hours in the barracks on a bunk together, whispering and giggling. I think we were all in shock that Julie could give up the macho officer for Edna, but I never heard of anyone complaining. The last I heard, they had moved to Seattle together after the war.

—  —  —

My conclusion is that during the war, with so much going on, it took more to upset us than lesbians, men groping us, and having to endure what is now called sexual harassment. We were losing our boys and maybe our freedom. Who cared about that unimportant stuff? To tell the truth, in most cases we took the "harassment" as a form of flattery.  Who knew?

## Love and Marriage

There were a few weddings among our crew.  It was easy to get married.
I think the motivation was to have someone to come home to.  One of my
closest friends, Janet, fell in love with a chief and married him in the chapel
on base.  I stood up for them.  Janet was from New Jersey, too – from up
north, as we say in that small, ridiculous state.  She had a smile and a way
about her that warmed your heart.  Her husband was a down-to-earth,
uncomplicated man, a good-natured soul, easy-going, and an all around
good guy.  They were perfect together.  Sometimes the magic works.  It was
a lovely wedding and it turned out to be a good marriage.  They were
deeply in love, stayed together, and had several children.

Naturally, we had a few pregnancies.  Those girls were simply discharged
and shipped home.  No room for babies on base.  That was a gigantic "no-no."

—    —    —

One of the men I dated was a cadet named Bill.  He looked like a Greek
God but came from Little Rock, where his father owned a hardware store.
Bill was blond, with a tan complexion, blue eyes, and pearly-white, perfect
teeth.  We dated for about a year, and when I was dating him, there were no
other men in my life.  We took our relationship seriously and remained true
to each other.  Yes, he had wanted to get married, but I didn't feel comfortable in those days making that kind of commitment.  There was too much
going on in the world, and we weren't sure what the future would be.  I was
smart enough to realize that just wearing a skirt might be the reason for all
the popularity.  Plus, I just couldn't picture living in Arkansas, raising a
family.  I had never been there and didn't even know for sure where it was.

My other major problem with Bill was that all my so-called friends would
hit on him.  I caught one of them fondling him under the table at dinner one
night in the Hotel Driscoll dining room.  I was furious!  He was mine, for
Pete's sake!  I didn't mind sharing perfume, hose, or laundry soap, but I
drew the line at my man!  That was quite a scene, but it had a strange ending.  That girl, a lovable redhead, remained a close friend, and Bill finally
graduated and flew away.

Shortly after he left, Bill called me from Jacksonville, where he was stationed after graduating.  The night he called I was on liberty at the Driscoll

Resplendent in our dress whites at a wedding. I am second girl from right.

Bill, the "Greek God."                    Tommy - Chief.

Hotel. A few friends had dropped by, and when the operator put him through to the room, a man answered the phone. We were all just hanging out, sitting around chatting. I didn't even know the guy who picked up the phone, but he considered it a big joke to infer that we were in bed together. Bill was convinced I was having an affair, and that was the end of our relationship. After the war ended and I was headed home, I went through Jacksonville and called Bill at the base, but he would have nothing to do with me. We would have had cute kids, though.

—     —     —

Then there was Tommy, a chief who was lots of fun. He was from Corpus, so he knew the town well. Tommy was tall, had curly black hair, a mischievous smile, and an air of gaiety about him. One advantage of being with him was that he knew all of the managers and owners of the local bars and restaurants. We received great service wherever we went. We also made it to a lot of local house parties, beach picnics, and "homey" type activities. That affair lasted six months. Then Tommy got shipped out.

Mert, a Marine pilot, was a real joker. Mert had a great sense of humor and was perhaps more fun to be with than any of the others. He was full of the blarney. He called himself "two-blanket Cameron." The officers who had cars usually put a blanket in the trunk for use on the beach during dates. He felt special having two in his trunk.

It was Mert who warned me that if I married a pilot, I should be willing to take second place to the airplane. That turned out to be so true! I did marry a pilot and was indeed second place, but thanks to Mert, I was aware of what it would be like before I went into the marriage.

We got stuck in Mert's car once when we parked on the beach and the tide came in. That was exciting. We had to wade in to shore, then have the car towed out of the bay. Another fine mess he got me in!

—     —     —

When my mother came to Texas to visit, I borrowed Mert's car to take her and a few of the WAVES over to Port Aransas for the day. Mert told me to check the oil and water every few miles. It was an old junker, so I believed him. We spent a lot of time in gas stations without finding anything wrong. I finally realized it was just Mert's idea of a joke. He went on to become a pilot with the Marine aerobatic team.

On that trip with my mother, she had such a good time. Mom had a camera with her and insisted that we take off our uniforms. She took pictures of us posing in the sand dunes with just our bras and panties on. They turned

Ollie, Helen, Janet and Bucky at Aransas Pass, Texas.

Bucky and I at Aransas Pass. Both photos taken by my mother.

out great and are still dear to me.

There was a short interlude when I dated a leftenant commander in charge of the English squadron on base. He came for me in a black limo, with the British flags flying on the front. Very impressive! One problem with that relationship was his expectation that I'd jump into the sack after one bottle of booze. I told my friends back in the barracks that it took at least two bottles! (just kidding…)

All was well until he wanted to introduce me to the European plan. This meant he'd supply me with an apartment in town, and I would be all his. My reaction to that proposition was extremely negative, so that ended that.

Theda fell in love with an officer who came from high society in San Francisco. He went on leave and came back married to an old girl friend from home who was also from the upper echelons of society. It broke Theda's heart. She went into a depression that lasted for several months. No dating or going into town; just staying on base in the barracks, consuming Mars bars and soda pop. I tried and tried to get her to come out and play, but it took time. Later, she met a Marine pilot named Dick, and again she was in love. He was shipped out to China to fly the Hump (the supply route to India over the Himalayas), and that put Theda back in the barracks.

The following tells what some of the men felt about dating us. I think it came out in a Corpus newspaper:

*I think I shall never rave*
*about another Navy WAVE,*

*A WAVE whose appetite's no fake,*
*Who orders caviar and steak,*

*A WAVE who looks at me with stars,*
*Then turns her head for silver bars,*

*A WAVE who must forever wear*
*Six inches chopped off her hair,*

*A WAVE who loves to stay out late*
*But can't be kissed at her front gate.*

*God, give me strength my love to save,*
*And never date another WAVE!*

Having dinner with Leftenant Commander Whatley.

Souvenir handkerchief from visit to Laredo, Mexico.

## Feelings

All the time we were in Corpus, we bitched and complained. We had to. In fact, it was almost mandatory. While there were many great things about being there, there were many hard and sad times, too. We lived with underlying feelings of fear and doom. We all knew during our first year of the war that things weren't going well. The Germans were bogged down in Russia, Americans had landed in North Africa to join the Brits, and the Japanese had been bloodied by the U.S. Navy at the Battle of Midway. But the Axis still controlled vast parts of the world. We felt sure of why we were fighting, but the struggle against such evil was taking its toll on our resources.

What would happen if we lost? Who would be in control of our country? What kind of a life would we have if indeed we lived to experience it? Would we be raped and tortured? Would we be imprisoned? In addition to feeling like we had to help those living under the jackboot, these were fears that motivated us to do all we could for our country and the war effort.

To talk openly about these feelings would have made them too real. They entered my mind at night after lights out and all was quiet, along with thoughts of home, family, old friends, and the life we'd led before Hitler, Mussolini, and Hirohito came into our lives.

The reality of what was happening in the outside world permeated our consciousness. The news of so many young men giving up their lives for our country and freedom was devastating. I got depressed and homesick. We were doing what we could, but it seemed like it wasn't enough. In some ways, it felt as if I were in another world and nothing was real or true. It was like living in a nightmare that wouldn't end. My way of coping was to stay active and concentrate on the daily routine.

The boys and men we associated with were shipped out for active duty. We knew their chances of staying alive were slim. Stories of horrific battles, abuse of prisoners of war, and all the bombing, shelling, and strafing our boys endured were overwhelming. We all had the underlying fear that the war would never end. We felt we were doomed to live and die in the Navy.

—   —   —

To be a woman and not allowed to be closer to the action was extremely frustrating. Sometimes I wished I'd been a nurse, but, to be honest, that thought paralyzed me with fear. To survive, I learned to escape into activity at work and force myself to be with others. We shared the same fears and emotional pain. I thank God we had each other's companionship.

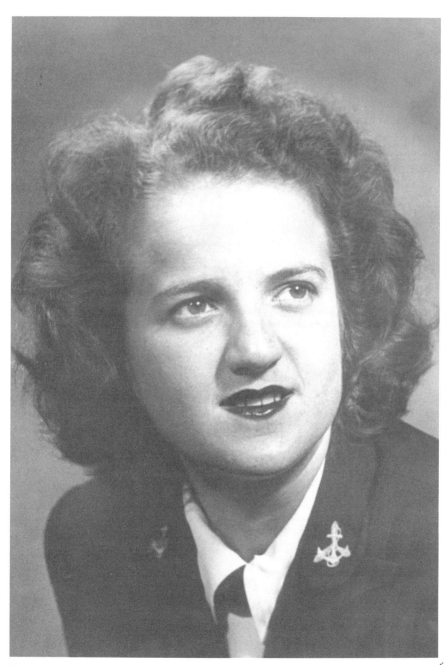

Portrait circa 1943.

## Meeting Our "First Lady"

Eleanor Roosevelt visited our base and that was quite a big deal for us. The main event as far as we were concerned was Mrs. Roosevelt's coming to our chow hall for lunch and giving a short talk. I will always remember how charming and gracious that lady was. While hardly a looker, she became beautiful in my eyes because of her charisma and manner of communicating.

We had a big parade for her. The WAVES drove dignitaries in official cars. I was assigned to the Mexican officials. We were required to drive slowly. They were safe with us, as we were well trained by then to obey orders.

## Shore Leave

We did get to go home on leave occasionally, and what a treat! Welcome-home parties, old familiar food, meals at Linton's and Horn & Hardart's in Philly, cinnamon buns, scrapple, and creamed chipped beef.

As good as it was to be back with family and friends, I realized that I was out of place in that environment. My friends from school were married and had small children. They'd followed the normal pattern and I had flown the coop. My life was on a totally different path from theirs. When I was with the girls from high school, they chatted about diapers, formula and babies. That was their world now and mine was still in the Navy. Even the ones whose husbands were in the service were living at home while their mates were overseas. In a way, it was a relief to go back to my familiar surroundings at Corpus with all my buddies.

When we went on leave, we were permitted to fly on military transport planes. On New Year's Day in 1944, I was fortunate to get a ride to New Orleans on a Navy plane. We flew over the Sugar Bowl game - a thrilling spectacle from the air. Downtown New Orleans was trashed from all the parties the night before. It looked like a ghost city. I traveled back to the base on crowded trains, packed solid with military personnel. I remember the ride through Texas always felt like a vast expanse of nothing, then Houston, then Corpus – total isolation from our former lives.

## Togetherness

Outside the south gate of the base there was a wonderful roadhouse called the Chicken Shack, run by a loving woman who called herself Mom Avery.

1st Anniversary Party at Mom Avery's Chicken Shack. Mom Avery is on the left.

*"Pistol-Packin' Momma"* theme party at Mom Avery's.

Our whole radio shack gang converged on it and had beer-guzzling contests. Each person had a case (yes, *a case*) of beer by his or her chair, and whoever finished first won. I don't remember what we won - probably one terrific hangover! I do remember the fried chicken was good.

We held a WAVE anniversary celebration at the Chicken Shack and tore the place apart. No men, just us letting our hair down, dancing and singing. The song *"Pistol Packing Mama"* was big then, so we took off our Navy ties, put them on like masks, and made like bandits. We were like a bunch of little kids, whooping it up! We'd grown to be a sisterhood – closer even than family.

We often hung out in the recreation room. The rec room was our main social gathering place and source of news. Most of our waking hours were spent there. We had no television in those days – just the radio for news and music. We read newspapers, magazines and books, and there was lots of conversation. There was always someone to talk to. We complained about work, Texas, the weather, the war and wanting to go home.

Our one telephone was there, as well as the candy and Coke machines. That phone was kept humming, lemme tell you. With about 150 girls, can you imagine how difficult it was to get on the damn thing, and how impossible it was for someone calling to get through?

We also did laundry and ironing in that area. We did lots of laundry, especially in the summer. It was commonplace to go back to barracks at noon to change our seersucker dresses, which became limp from the humidity.

Many famous last lines were heard in the rec room, such as:

*"If I get a telephone call, tell them I'll be in the wash house."*

*"Tonight I'm going to bed early!"*

*"Any Cokes in the machine?"*

*"I can't. I've got the duty."*

*"Who's going to Ship's Service? Bring me…(whatever)."*

*"And if she isn't there, she must be in the head."*

*"What's for chow?"*

*"Whatcha got in the package?"*

*"Can I borrow five until payday?"*

*"I was supposed to be in town an hour ago."*

*"Got any nickels?"*

*"I met a guy on the bus."*

*"Can I borrow a cigarette? I left mine at work."*

And the saying that takes the prize…..

*"Wouldn't you like to stand by for me next Saturday night?"*

## The Wild Blue Yonder

On one particularly gorgeous day, a Navy mail pilot invited me to go on the mail run to our adjoining bases. This was strictly taboo. The Navy had banned us from single engine planes. They didn't think a female with a parachute would have the courage to jump in an emergency. How about that for discrimination? That's the way it was before women's liberation.

In spite of, or because of this, I donned coveralls and a sailor hat and jumped into the back seat of an SNJ, and away we went. SNJs were often used as trainers, and had tandem cockpits with a long Plexiglas™ cover, so the view was great. Naturally, he wanted to show off, so we did loops and spins. I loved it. We were skydiving through those fleecy clouds and chasing them all over. What a day that was!

The only negative thing about the trip was that after landing back at the base, I lost my breakfast. I think it was the first time that I experienced "projectile vomiting."

## Transition

In November of 1943 I was transferred to Air Traffic Control on the main base. This office was located on the ground floor of a hangar, centrally located at our main airport. It was interesting duty. We handled all the flight plans for incoming and outgoing flights. This gave me the opportunity to meet and talk to admirals, Army Air Corps pilots, and our own Navy guys going on cross-country flights.

To be able to be in direct contact with those daring young men in their flying machines was a dream come true. I had such admiration for pilots. To me, they were almost super-human - so debonair, self-confident, and carefree. It was an honor and a privilege to work with and around them.

We handled flight plans, gave the pilots weather conditions, and kept track of their flights. We had telephone contact with our other bases and an air-to-ground position for radio communication. We were in direct contact with the squadrons of cadets who were checking the flight board and weather and preparing to take off into the wild blue. Exciting, to say the least.

We watched the planes taxiing and taking off, doing their "touch and go's," lining up for formation flying, and practicing for aircraft carrier operations. It was awesome for me to be on the flight line and in direct contact with this phase of the training activity.

—      —      —

But it wasn't all fun and games. It was painful when a plane was reported overdue and not heard from. We all knew that the chances of hearing good news about a missing plane were very slim.

We weren't in combat, but we did lose a lot of gallant young men. These accidents, so very close to home, along with news of battles not going well in the Pacific and the European theaters, could make us very depressed.

—      —      —

My fondest memory of this period is of going on duty at dawn as the sun was rising, walking through rows and rows of training planes starting up their engines for the day's flights. It was totally thrilling, a concert of power being unleashed with a background of a new day appearing in magnificent color patterns. I should mention, though, that you had to watch where you walked; a propeller in motion could certainly ruin your day!

—      —      —

One morning, I was on the air-to-ground radio's local frequency, listening to the pilots who were training. It was dawn and the sun was rising in a clear and spectacular sky. On the air came this voice singing, *"Oh, What a Beautiful Morning."* It certainly was. I guess he just had to let it out.

I loved it when our Mexican pilots were up. Just like their personalities, the chatter was excitable, constant, and fun to listen to. You could just picture them totally enjoying the freedom of flight.

This experience led me to ask to be transferred to duty at the Sea Plane Tower. Having had a taste of being in contact with flying and fliers, I wanted more. This duty was wonderful. We were on the fourth floor of a tower where we could observe both the bay and the hangars alongside the water.

The seaplanes were clumsy-looking compared to the fighter training planes. They had big bellies which made them look pregnant. When they took off, skimming along the top of the water and lumbering into the sky, they resembled big beautiful shore birds.

Our duty in the tower was to keep an eye on the activity and give radio permission for taxiing and take off and landing procedures. It was exciting to be a part of this operation and very different from my other assignments.

While there, I was given a night ride on a PBY Catalina, a Navy seaplane. This was a large, lumbering plane for long, over-the-water flights, and therefore had bunks as well as seats. It turned into quite an adventure. That was the night that I became a member of the then-exclusive "Mile-High Club." It is one of my more prestigious accomplishments. On the off-chance you are not familiar with this phrase, it is simply having sex in an airplane, mid-air.

It has become more popular in the years following, with the bathroom being the most common site for such action. Not easy, but do-able. I suppose having had a bunk for our activity would be considered luxurious. It was a challenge for us to do it with the flight crew up front, but I don't think we really cared.

That particular officer was a Lt. Commander, a duty officer at the Sea Plane Tower. We had strong chemistry, the kind where you feel the electricity flowing between you. He was due to go on the PBY that night, and after we shared a few drinks in the tower, he invited me to go along. Now, all of this was breaking every rule in the Navy, but it was well worth the risk. I still remember his name, where he was from, and what he looked like. He was tall, with black hair, dark eyes, and a charming smile. He had a great personality and sense of humor. I even recall him saying that I had the roundest heels in the Navy. They didn't give out medals for that. I'm sure the sex was spectacular, but at my age it is just a fond memory.

I never did understand completely, but there was a conflict about my leaving Communications – some sort of turf battle between some of the department heads. I was shipped out to Pensacola, Florida, probably around January of 1945. Coincidentally, Theda was shipped out with me. As I recall, we were labeled "trouble makers." What could they possibly have meant?

## Pensacola

The most interesting thing on our train ride from Corpus Christi to Pensacola, Florida, happened in the middle of the night. Theda was in the lower bunk and after a short train stop, I was awakened by her shaking me and yelling, *"Johnny, get up!"* It seems she woke up and found a hot hamburger lying on her pillow. We took it to the ladies' room and after much speculation as to how it got there, and whether it was poisoned, we ended up saying what the hell, and ate it. We never did solve that mystery. By the way, it was good!

Theda and I were assigned to the radio shack. Back to the world of dit-dah. During our stint of duty there, we stayed on base most of the time. We had good beaches not too far from our barracks. The beaches in Pensacola were even whiter than those in Corpus and the water was aqua blue and warm. We went out on the bay on boat trips with the gang we worked with, fishing or just cruising. We did go to a few parties in town, but not many.

I fell in love with our chief in the radio shack, who happened to be married. He was tall, thin, blond, totally appealing to me, and it was mutual. It never developed, though. Theda helped hold me back on that one, but I sure lusted after him. That may have had a lot to do with our staying on base. I had my stalking to do, and Theda had to keep tabs on me. I had to content myself with just being around him, and it wasn't easy. Thank God I recovered from that obsession when the war ended. Raging hormones…

On the base there was a float out in the bay at the beach. To reach it required a short swim through deep water. How many times did Theda darn near drown me on that trip? She could swim, but not too well, and often panicked and grabbed me. I will say, it was a useful way to meet rescuers, now that I think about it. Maybe she was a better swimmer than she pretended to be, who knows?

## V-J Day

While in Pensacola, we saw many films about the war action … extremely graphic and difficult to watch. It made the war real – too real. D-Day, June 6, 1944, had given us some glimmer of hope. The following year, V-E Day came and went, leaving "only" Japan to deal with. It was commonly held that the Japanese would fight on until the last, and that the war could go on indefinitely. This would mean years of continuous loss of life on both sides. The culture of Japan was based on not "losing face," and to them surrender was worse than death. The military ruled Japan, and they were determined to fight to the end.No one knew just how we were going to invade Japan.

At the beginning of August, a message came through on our teletype about a bomb having been dropped. It was quickly denied, and we were told it was a mistake. August 6, 1945 came, however, and with it the news that an atomic bomb had been dropped on Hiroshima. We weren't sure if it was true. It was verified, and three days later we dropped a second bomb on Nagasaki. Japan soon surrendered and the war was over.

—       —       —

Our first reaction was utter jubilation. We had won! We had survived! We could go home! But soon our excitement was tempered by the realization of the horrible consequences of our having dropped the bombs - the death of hundreds of thousands of innocent civilians. In the larger picture, it did stop the war, but was it worth it to be that inhumane?

I have never understood man's cruelty to man, or been able to make peace with it. This, of course, is simply my recollection of that time, and these are just my personal views.

The entire country went crazy with joy and festivity on V-J Day. We, on the other hand, were restricted to base. We celebrated by gorging on chocolate ice cream and potato chips. That was our usual answer to stress. We were all roaming around the barracks and base. Yes, delighted that the war was over, but in a way feeling a loss of identity. What now? We'd been living this life for three years. I always say the Navy got the best years of my life, or at least the cream of my youth.

—       —       —

Theda and I tentatively made plans to stay together; we'd become like sisters and couldn't even think of parting. Our goal was to go to California, get jobs, and see what life was like "out West." We had no idea when we'd be discharged or how we would reach these goals, but we both knew in our hearts there was no way we could go back to our pre-war lifestyle.

We had matured during the last years and had to move on. The Navy had taught us to be self sufficient and had opened our eyes to a world much bigger than our small towns in West Virginia and New Jersey. We wanted adventure, and felt ready to go for it.

## Getting Out

The personnel office began issuing information about releasing the military, and we started receiving messages about how it would take place. We were being classified according to rank, length of service, etc.

Naturally, Theda and I figured we'd be among the first out. We were the first in, so why not the first out? I was down at the beach one day when Theda appeared, all excited, and said she'd heard over the loudspeaker in the barracks that we were to report to the personnel office the next morning.

—　—　—

I remember being a little confused - it was so fast. It was perhaps August 21, and I hadn't seen any written notices. Knowing the Navy and how they operate, however, I knew we'd better be there. When we reported the next morning, I noticed the office was packed with chiefs. The clerk wanted to know why we were there.

Theda could be very distracting, convincing, and manipulative. Most men melted around her. She made the clerk believe we were definitely being discharged, due to our seniority. Although we were the first WAVES he had encountered, he reluctantly got out the necessary papers with a list of check-out offices to visit, and away we went!

We went to many different offices and kept getting the same reaction, like *"Oh, we didn't know they were discharging WAVES yet."* But we had the forms, so in typical Navy fashion, they just kept signing us out.

—　—　—

When we arrived at the medical office, the doctor informed us they were absolutely not discharging females and furthermore, they weren't set up for that yet. Upon seeing our partially signed papers, however, he told us to come back the next morning. We did, and he signed us off, too. This was the story at every stop - disbelief, but going along just the same with finalizing our discharge. In all fairness, it was a chaotic and confusing time for everyone, so soon after V-J Day.

On arrival at personnel, our last place to appear, the female Ensign on duty went into orbit. She really lost it and turned purple, screaming at us, *"What are you two doing here again? You always were trouble makers!"* She finally calmed down enough to tell us to sit down and wait. Wow, we thought, this is it – shot at dawn, or worse.

After about ten minutes, she came back with a male officer who informed her that she was wasting her breath. She was yelling at civilians. We were officially out!

—　—　—

All our discharge papers were signed, sealed, and delivered. All we needed was our mustering-out pay and we were gone. It was August 24, 1945.

Now, during this entire period, we kept noticing that the only other people who were checking out were old Navy chiefs, with hash-marks up their

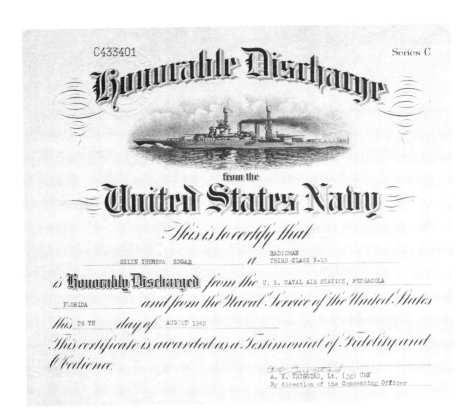

C433401  Series C

# Honorable Discharge

## from the

## United States Navy

*This is to certify that*

HELEN THERESA EDGAR     *a*     RADIOMAN
THIRD CLASS V-10

*is* **Honorably Discharged** *from the* U. S. NAVAL AIR STATION, PENSACOLA

FLORIDA *and from the Naval Service of the United States*

*this* 24 TH *day of* AUGUST 1945

*This certificate is awarded as a Testimonial of Fidelity and Obedience.*

A. E. THYGSTAD, Lt. (jg) USN
By direction of the Commanding Officer

My final discharge papers.

Free at Last!  The night we got out of the Navy.  Theda is on the left.

sleeves indicating long-time service. However, we thought we were special. I guess we were. We got ourselves honorably discharged, totally illegally!

Before giving us our discharge pay, however, they did plead with us to go quietly into the night, not to talk to the press, to just go home! After a night celebrating in town, in civvies, of course, we were delighted to board a train and do just that.

I returned to Collingswood, where banners all over the house said "Welcome Home," and where I attended many Victory parties. Then I had to tell everyone that I was leaving again. I don't think my mother ever forgave me for that. She'd purchased strawberry jelly and cheddar cheese especially for me, and I wasn't staying to eat it. I was off to California with my friend Theda.

## Reflections

I want to conclude this part by sharing a few thoughts about my life in the Navy and where it led me. My tour of duty in the Armed Services gave me self-esteem and confidence. It taught me how to share and care. The years I spent during the war, wearing the uniform and being a part of that magnificent group of men and women, are, and always will be, the proudest and most satisfactory part of my life.

To this day, I am still overwhelmed with feelings of patriotism and true allegiance to my country. While watching a parade, the return of servicemen from overseas, a military funeral, the ceremony of "colors," or military planes flying overhead, I experience feelings that literally bring me to tears. When I visit air bases, I become nostalgic and almost envious of the personnel who are still living that life style.

In a strange way, it was similar to being in the womb. We were cared for and protected, fed, clothed, and housed. We lived in our own world and we had each other. We didn't even have to make decisions. What a way to live!

—     —     —

We were but a small cog in the wheel of the war effort, but we had the personal satisfaction of knowing that we played a role and did our part. We went through tragedy and sorrow, and worked and played hard. We were as one, together through turmoil and victory, which gave us a sense of unity. My hope and prayer is that some day, some way, our country can be as one again, without needing a war to accomplish that unity.

# Part IV

# Post-War Challenges

## California, Here We Come

As I said, Theda and I had many discussions as to what we'd do after the war, and where we wanted to live. We both wanted to continue in communications, preferably at an airport, and agreed that California would be ideal.

Theda went to the Civil Aeronautics Administration (CAA) in Washington, D.C., to get some information on job availability. That was typical Theda - don't mess around, go right to the top. She was told that the prospects were dim, but that a guy named Cap, the head of the CAA in Santa Monica, had a soft spot for females and would be the best possibility for us.

That worked for us, since California was exactly where we were headed. We'd heard many stories about the beauty of that state - how you could go skiing in the mountains and swimming at the beach on the same day, and this was long before freeways!

I went to West Virginia for a few days to join up with Theda. It was interesting. Her parents' house had been re-located about a city block down and across the street by a tornado, so the plumbing wasn't hooked up yet.

This meant we had to go to an uncle's house for our baths. There was a hole in the bathroom wall where we knew he watched us, but we figured he had earned a look for the free bath.

He was a happy country soul, content with his life in the mountains of West Virginia. The drinking he did in the local bar was his only social life. He was a confirmed bachelor and satisfied with that status.

Hospitality in the mountains of West Virginia was overkill. I arrived about 2 am. by train and was greeted by Theda's parents. They were the sweetest older couple and treated me like royalty. Her mom had a fried chicken dinner set out on the dining room table, with mashed potatoes, biscuits, the works, fresh from the kitchen. They were typical old-fashioned folk, with hearts of gold, oozing love. After a few days of being spoiled rotten, we departed. Many tears flowed, but good wishes went with us.

We took the train to Dayton, Ohio, and went to Wright-Patterson Air Field. Somebody told us that perhaps we could get a free airplane ride to California. We put on our WAVES uniforms and removed our "lame duck" emblems that we were given to show that we weren't on active duty. Theda conned our way on base where we stayed overnight in the WAAC barracks.

How she did this and got away with it, I'll never know. I do know that when we went on base, she kept batting her blue eyes and talking with that thick southern accent. The poor guard never did ask us for our identification or papers. The WAAC barracks had bunks for visitors, and there again they accepted us without question.

The next morning we went to the flight service area and listed ourselves for a ride. The first one available was a B-24 bomber to Clovis, New Mexico. Not as far as California, but certainly further west than Ohio. After takeoff, about one hour into the flight, the pilot discovered we were not active duty. He came down from the cockpit to the "bubble" where we were and wanted to throw us off the plane. He was very upset, yelling, *"Don't you two realize I could be court-martialed for this?"* We assured him that if he didn't crash, we wouldn't tell, and if he did crash, who cared? He was satisfied with our logic. The remainder of the trip went well.

We sat below the cockpit in the Plexiglas™ bubble, Theda knitting away while I just enjoyed the scenery. It was a delightful ride. Neither of us had ever seen the rest of the country, so it was a new and mind-boggling experience, especially from our vantage point.

From New Mexico, we took the train into Los Angeles. That train trip also proved to be different. It was so crowded that Theda and I had to share a bottom bunk. We were no longer separated from the men. During the night, I was awakened by a hand groping around my breast. I opened the curtain and shouted at a very drunk soldier to go away, get some sleep, and leave me alone. A few minutes later, back came the hand. This time, I grabbed the wrist and yelled for Theda to pull the cord for the conductor. We were parked on a siding, waiting until morning to allow other trains to pass. All hell broke loose and they removed the soldier from the train.

An officer came by next morning to see if I wanted to press charges. Naturally, I didn't. He was a married man and scared to death. I just told the officer to tell him to go home to his wife.

We finally made it into Los Angeles. Theda had an elderly aunt and uncle in Santa Monica so we headed there. They were very good to us, but didn't waste any time helping us find a room to rent. They made every effort to entertain us the best they could. They took us on a trip to Chino, which was way out in the country back then. I'll bet they were one happy couple when they saw the door close on our butts. I'm sure having us as house guests upset their routine.

My strongest memory from that visit was a trip to a supermarket. I think it was a Ralph's. So big, clean, and full of fresh produce. I had never seen anything like it.

Theda and I had been through thick and thin together, and we had become very close. It seemed to me that she was always getting into trouble and taking me with her. I always felt that she attracted all the men in our lives. Years later, I discovered she felt it was I who was the popular and dynamic member of the team, and she was the one who just trailed along.

Perhaps that was the basis for the true friendship we'd developed, each of us in awe of the other's qualities. Neither of us had a sister, and we became closer than family over the years. We wore the same size clothes, so had a "joint" wardrobe. That included shoes. Even our feet were the same size.

At this time, we were really broke. We applied for, and got, the 52/50 allotment (52 weeks at $50 a week) to help us readjust to civilian life. The critical shortage of housing during the war continued for several years afterwards, and so the pickings were slim. We found a room in a shack in Santa Monica, across the street from the back of the Miramar Hotel. It was a lovely street with nice houses.

Our rental was a small guest house in the rear of one of the homes. We would saunter down the street as if we lived in one of the nice houses, look around to make sure no one was watching, then make a mad dash down the driveway to our shack.

Our place consisted of three bedrooms, one bath, and a kitchen, which all six tenants shared. We had no bedding, so we slept on the mattress in our Navy overcoats. None of the walls were soundproof, so we all knew everyone else's business. At times we heard noises we'd rather not have had to listen to. I always felt like I'd get athlete's foot or some dreaded disease from taking a shower. The kitchen was old and dirty, so we avoided using it.

We found a friendly bar at 4th and Broadway called the Tahiti and hung out there a lot. Being a female in a bar meant that we never had to pay for our drinks. Johnny, the bartender at the Tahiti, became our new best friend. He'd point out military men who were passing through. We came on to them, and eventually suggested a restaurant we knew for dinner. After we'd eaten and a reasonable time had elapsed, we excused ourselves, went to the ladies' room, climbed out the window, and ran like hell for our shack, bellies full.

### Discrimination

We were well aware that we needed to find work. Employment was a little tight in those days for females. Most of the kind of work we'd done during the war was now considered inappropriate for women, and they wanted to get rid of us, not hire us.

When we first arrived in Santa Monica, we went to the CAA and applied for teletype or radio positions at an airport. Although we were veterans, Cap, the head of that department, informed us that he had no positions available. He said that he'd keep us on file. We knew that meant the "circular file," and that they had no intention of hiring us.

It was 1945. We had served in the Navy for thirty-four months and proved that we were capable of doing communications work. We knew that the airports and communications stations had the type of jobs we wanted, but we ran into the same old roadblock. When I look back, I realize how difficult it has been for women (and still is, to some extent) to break through the barriers of the male world. I also can see the effect that World War II had on women's equality.

—    —    —

In my youth, women were expected to stay at home, marry a nice local boy, and settle down to raise a family. It was a shock to our families and communities when we broke ranks and didn't conform to that expectation. Outwardly, our families praised and supported us because of the war. Underneath were the rumors concerning our motivation. We were suspect as to our morality and chastity. "Good girls" didn't leave home. It was just not done. Surely we could have found patriotic duties locally. There were the factories, the Red Cross - anything but the military! That was for men only!

Today, when I see women standing tall in uniform, side by side with the men in all areas of the military world, I gloat with pride. I know those of us who were willing to dare entering the male world had a small part in achieving equality. I feel like saying to each and every one of them, *"U Go, Girl!"*

There was a time when we considered joining the union and becoming cocktail waitresses. The money was good and we sure did need it. This might be hard to believe, but we were both afraid our parents would find out and would disapprove. That should tell you something about early upbringing and the effect it has.

We filed for unemployment compensation at the State Employment Office. Theda found a job in Hollywood as a receptionist at a studio in the make-up department. I had cleverly listed my qualifications as Sea Plane Tower Operator and Radio Operator, so there were no available jobs for me.

I hung out at the Tahiti for a few months and drew unemployment checks. One day when I was at the Unemployment Office picking up my check, the manager of the Employment Office came out and said he wanted to see me. He'd looked up my previous experience and hired me to work in that office. I had to take the job or my unemployment status would have been canceled. The party was over. I went to work.

While working at the Employment Office, I checked back with Cap at least once a week. He was friendly, but still said that there were no jobs. One day one of my co-workers at the employment office brought me a notice of positions open for radio operators at a few airports. I went sailing back to Cap and used the veteran status as leverage.

Cap said he'd consider us if we could pass a Morse code test. What he didn't realize was that this was the one thing we could do, almost in our sleep. We took the darned test, passed it, and were hired.

Cap later confided that he had orders after the war to try to get rid of females in his department and obviously had no intention of hiring new ones. He even admitted having thrown our original applications in the wastebasket as we left his office.

Most of the available jobs were in California (Blythe and Needles) and Fallon, Nevada. These were all small desert towns, cut off from civilization in any form. No way did we want to be out in the desert after our years in Texas and Florida. Thank God, the Oakland airport was also available. We decided to go to Oakland, as neither of us had been to San Francisco, and we figured why not?

## Oakland

We again found a crummy one-bedroom apartment, in an old two-story house on 14th Street in Oakland. It wasn't a good neighborhood, even in those days. We had to take a trolley and a bus to the airport. Our apartment was upstairs, hanging off the back end of the old frame house. It consisted of one bedroom, a large kitchen, and a made-over closet that was the bathroom. You had to know what you planned to do before you entered the bath - two choices, either shower or use the john. Washing our faces and brushing our teeth was done at the kitchen sink. Pure luxury.

Two gay guys had lived in the apartment prior to our arrival. They had relocated one floor below us, for more space. One was short and fat, the other tall and lean. The bed we slept in had been theirs, and we'd go into fits of giggling when thinking about them in our bed. The mattress sagged so badly we had to hang on the sides of the darn thing to keep from rolling onto each other.

This apartment became the hangout and stopover for the Air Force flight service officers at the airport, plus the air traffic controllers and communicators we worked with. Once again, we threw some pretty good parties.

One payday, Theda and I headed for San Francisco on the good old "A" train and got a room at the St. Francis Hotel. It was difficult to get out of the bathtub after all our grimy showers in our post-war rentals.

Our work at the Oakland airport was similar to what we did while in the Navy. We didn't use Morse code, but we did operate the teletype and an air-to-ground radio set up. We handled all the military and civilian flight plans. The pilots either came into the office to file the flight plan and check the weather, or phoned in from other locations. We kept track of them until they arrived at their destinations. If one turned up missing, the Civil Air Patrol was notified and the search would begin. We hated to call the Civil Air Patrol. It's hard to believe, but it was not uncommon to lose one or two of them, in addition to the missing plane.

Our office was adjacent to the weather bureau. We sent and transmitted weather conditions on the teletype. We also broadcast the local weather on the air every thirty minutes. Another duty was to send and receive the teletype messages. We had miles of messages on the mid-watch from CAA in Washington regarding mechanical difficulties. That was scary, but not when one considered the number of airplanes and flights each day.

–       –       –

At this time I decided to take flying lessons. I could get them through the G.I. Bill because I'd worked with airplanes. The nearest flight school was at the Hayward airport, not too far from Oakland where I signed up. What an adventure!

First, I couldn't conceive of the idea that the wind under the wing kept the airplane up. I dug in, however, and eventually logged about 28 hours flying solo. I could take off like a bird – I just pushed the throttle full ahead and the thing took off on its own. I really think the only thing that saved me from self-destruction was that Piper Cub, a most forgiving plane.

After awhile I learned the landmarks and what action to take at each one. For instance, a water tower – pull throttle back some, the salt field – pull some knob out. I'd land that plane no matter what. On approach, I'd be so scared my legs would cramp up and paralyze. There I'd be, massaging my calves, trying to get that little devil on the ground. Not once did I consider going around. Well, that led to some pretty weird and scary landings.

Most of the time I simply dropped the plane to the runway, bounced several times, and there I was, on the ground. One time I missed the runway completely and landed out in the middle of the field, and got stopped by a big rock under one wheel. I got out and waited under the wing to be rescued. I just couldn't seem to find the airports from the air. The nicest thing they put in my logbook was that I made good recoveries from bad landings.

—        —        —

Another thing they frowned upon was my practicing spins out over San Francisco Bay. It looked friendly and soft to me. I was told if I went down, it would be like hitting a concrete wall. I could do spins well – just put the plane into a stall and let go of everything. The plane went into the spin maneuver and recovered on its own. It was a rush and really fun to do.

When it was past normal time for me to fly solo cross-country, the instructor signed off on me. I was a little hesitant to try, but the flight school needed the money and they were also willing to let me try. However, the manager of the airport intervened and begged them and me not to do it, so I dropped out. It was just as well. At least I am alive to tell the tale.

—        —        —

During this period, Theda's Marine pilot, Buttons (Dick), returned from China. What a scene that was. Theda had put on a few extra pounds since he left Corpus Christi for China. She went berserk trying to get thin in about three days – steam baths, massage, no food, and a new black suit to hide the weight.

What she seemed to forget was that he'd been way out in the boonies, and she'd look good to him no matter what. After a few days, we all went to Monterey where they got married. They took off for Cherry Point, North Carolina. That was hard on me. As I said, we wore each other's clothes, so I not only lost my best friend, but half my wardrobe went with her.

—        —        —

Luckily, I worked with two other girls at the airport who were looking for a place to live. We rented a nice apartment in San Leandro, close by the airport. Another WAVE, Lorie, showed up from Corpus Christi, pregnant by our Chief in the radio shack. This was a real shocker to me. I had no idea they'd had any kind of relationship. He was married, and we all knew and loved his wife.

Lorie was an attractive redhead and loved to party. It was after Theda and I moved to Pensacola that she got involved with Monty. There was no way she would ruin his life, let alone tell his wife. She simply left Corpus without telling the chief she was pregnant. He never found out.

She put the baby girl up for adoption. Lorie never forgave herself. She regretted giving up her baby, but felt at the time it was better for the child. On a trip to visit me a few years later, she shared with me that not a day went by that she didn't think about that baby and wonder how and where she was. I suppose we pay the price for our transgressions. Later, she met and married a Navy lieutenant commander, and left Oakland.

## Winslow, Arizona

Time passed. I got a promotion from GS5 (Government Service) to GS6, but had to move to Winslow, Arizona to get the upgrade. Winslow is a small railroad town. The airport took care of Trans-World Airlines flights, which had the only ticket counter. Our radio station was at the rear of the airport terminal. We had a counter for private pilots and pilots of non-scheduled airline flights to file flight plans and receive weather reports.

We were a tight-knit group of airport employees. We had to be. The folks in town had lived there forever, and the Indians were out on their reservation, so we were on our own. The area's biggest event was an Indian pow-wow, held once a year.

We had a lot of potluck dinners. The group also gathered in the local bowling alley. There was a creek outside of town in Rock Canyon where we went swimming. The water was ice cold, and locals warned us that it was dangerous. Several people had drowned in it. Snakes were plentiful, but when it got hot and dry in Arizona, we got desperate and climbed down the canyon over steep rocks and jumped in. Actually, the snakes never bothered us. They just swam along with us.

—    —    —

A private pilot who owned a jewelry store in town hung around the airport a lot. His name was Ernie. He had a beautiful Beechcraft Bonanza which he used to fly mercy flights to Phoenix, and he gave us rides at times. He took me down through the Grand Canyon one day, and what a spectacular flight that was. He was such a good soul but had a sad story and was lonesome.

He was from Chicago, where he'd had a business for years. He was married and had two small girls. His wife started to have mental problems, and her doctor advised Ernie to take her to a small town, away from stress. They packed a mobile home and headed for Arizona. When Ernie arrived in Winslow, he decided it would be perfect for her. He had to return to Chicago for his watch and jewelry repair equipment and left her with the children. After he was gone, she really lost it and tied the two girls to a bed and set fire to the trailer. Her family blamed Ernie. He was devastated and miserable about what happened to his family. Between grief and guilt, he was a lost soul. Our airport and the gang who worked there were his only social life. I think being in the airplane and off the face of the earth was the only place he got any peace.

Eventually, the isolation of the place got to me, and I went crawling back to Cap in Santa Monica, begging to be let out of purgatory. I took a voluntary step back to my old status GS5 and transferred to the Los Angeles airport. It was worth it.

## The Man of My Dreams

Our radio station was under Mike Lyman's bar and restaurant, at the old L.A. airport. After duty in Winslow, it was a busy, active environment. We worked the usual shifts around the clock, at times not taking lunch or dinner breaks. It was challenging and interesting, and I really loved going to work.

We had so many celebrities coming and going, some of us spent our lunch hour at one of the terminals, just to people-watch. We were there when Sinatra had a fight with the airport photographer, and saw Dean Martin and Jerry Lewis leaving for a trip – it was fun and exciting. Just watching everyone saying *"Hello"* and *"Goodbye"* was fascinating, always a lot of emotion.

I became friendly with Mike, who worked at Air Research, on the other side of the field. He handled flight plans for the corporate pilots using Air Research. They dealt with customizing airplanes for executives of large corporations. We talked on the phone frequently.

Mike built me a model airplane. He called one evening when I was working 1600 to midnight and told me it was ready and to come pick it up. While I was there, a Western Airlines pilot and a stewardess pulled up. He was a friend of Mike's, and we all ended up going across the street to

Patmar's, a restaurant and bar.

The pilot's name was Charley, or Chuck. He drove a wood-paneled, dark-green Ford convertible. He was in his uniform with a stewardess on his arm and looked mighty good to me. I set my sights on him and decided to try to get to know him.

One night Mike called me and said Chuck was home, needed some cheering up, and that I should call him. Seems he'd had a fight with his current girl friend and was feeling sad. I called and he asked if he could come over. I was on my way to a card game with friends and invited him to join us.

We never made it to the card game. He took me to a strip joint in Gardena because he wanted me to see Ginger, one of the strippers. She was a knockout. That started our relationship. We laughed about our first date for many years.

—    —    —

Chuck was 6 foot 4 inches, good-looking, and my favorite thing – a pilot. He had sandy hair, freckles and blue-gray eyes. Between trips for the airline, Chuck lived at home in Hawthorne. What I liked best about him was his respect for his family. He had a mother, sister, and brother, and acknowledged them. Most men in Los Angeles never mentioned family. I'm afraid some of them may have been hatched under a rock.

Chuck was of German and Scottish heritage and came from a background of male dominance. He served in the Marines on the USS North Carolina during the war. They were involved in the battle of the Solomon Islands, Guadalcanal, and other South Pacific action. A man's man.

After our infamous first date, we began seeing each other regularly. When he knew I was on duty, he'd call me on the air-to-ground radio when he was on approach. I knew instinctively that he was the one I'd been waiting for. At that point in time, before meeting Chuck, I had decided to move back home to New Jersey, and a little later had given notice at my job. I proposed to Chuck by telling him that either we got married or I was gone. How's that for romantic? It was the middle of December in 1950 when we met, and we married on the evening of Friday, March 9, 1951. What a wedding it was!

—    —    —

We hired a little chapel at 80th and Figuero Streets in South Los Angeles. By now, I think it is considered to be in the "hood," not an upper class neighborhood. We had plastic flowers and canned organ music. Just a few friends from the airport and his family attended. His mother sobbed loudly throughout the ceremony and almost had to be carried out when it was over

– she was losing her baby boy. The reception was in a bar across the street. Elegance beyond belief, but a day to remember. This magical moment was followed by our heading for Ensenada, Mexico, for a weekend honeymoon. We both had to be back Monday to go to work. We got as far as Laguna Beach and liked it so much that we simply stayed there.

This was still the age of women belonging in the kitchen, raising the children, and taking care of the house. Men were the providers and caretakers. Women's Lib will hate me for this, but I liked some aspects of it then and still do! It felt good to have a man take care of me. Chuck was truly masculine, 6′4″ tall as I said, so he was great to take to Disneyland. He was always easy to find in a crowd.

–    –    –

Given his German background, his Marine Corps stint, and later his career as an airline pilot, for me it was like trying to live with God. I had to be really clever and learn how to manipulate him in order to get my way. With a few years practice and my Navy training, I did quite well.

Probably as a result of his Marine Corps background he was meticulously neat in all areas. His bureau drawers were arranged to perfection; socks rolled and lined up, underwear folded and in stacks. I'm afraid my Navy training didn't leave me with the same organizational talent. When I opened a bureau drawer, the stuff was likely to fly out at me. I think opposites attract, and we sure were!

–    –    –

When I look back on those years, I realize we hardly ever discussed the war. I do remember while on a trip with him to Hawaii, we went to the Punchbowl Memorial. When he stood there reading the names of friends and lovingly ran his fingers over their names, he lost control and openly sobbed. I'd never seen him show that kind of raw emotion.

It was a solemn moment for both of us. It became clear to me that his memories were too painful to share. I simply held his hand and remained respectfully silent.

–    –    –

One aspect of my relationship with Chuck that frustrated me was his attitude about my service in the Navy as a WAVE. In that day and age, there were still strong feelings regarding male/female roles, and I think he was even a little ashamed of my having been a "sailor." He pointed out that we were only *"reserve and not really Navy."* He got extremely annoyed if I made any reference to it. I was very proud of my role during the war, so of course that made me angry.

I learned early on in our marriage not to discuss this particular subject too much. I will admit to having brought it up now and then just to get something started. We could always laugh at ourselves when getting too deep into disagreements. That was one of the many things I loved about him.

—     —     —

After the war, Chuck had taken flying lessons under the G.I. Bill then in effect for veterans. He also took the GED course to get his diploma for high school. With diligence and hard work, he progressed from visual flight rules to instruments. His first flying job was as a flight instructor, then he flew on non-scheduled airlines. He had many stories about those years, such as ending up in New York City, not adequately dressed for the cold weather, and having to sell blood to buy food on the layover.

It was a long, hard struggle for him to become an airline pilot with his limited education and experience. He was hired on a temporary basis in July 1949 by Western Airlines. After the war, the airlines had their pick of returning military pilots, but hired Chuck because of his youth and enthusiasm. He remained with Western until his death in 1979.

*"Okay, Girls, Man Your Bunks!"*

# Part V

# Love, Marriage, Kids
# and all that stuff

## The Dark Side...Helen

Now we come to the most difficult part of my life for me to share. I am not proud of the years that followed my marriage, but I am aware of how very sick I was. I suppose the bottom line is that we do the best we can, or know how to, at any given time of our lives.

What I didn't know, and didn't realize, was that slowly and methodically I had become an alcoholic. All the signs were there. I've learned to recognize them since recovery, but I had no clue then that I had a problem.

During the war years and even in my late teens there was a lot of drinking going on. As I've already shared, during my childhood and teen years I was a totally insecure person. I realize now that it was the way I saw it, not necessarily the way it really was. What I did know was that alcohol made me pretty, popular, a comedian, a good dancer, and one of the "gang." I fit in! I belonged!

I also know that I hated the party to end, the bars to close, and to have to go home to the real world. I experienced blackouts back then, but figured that anyone who drank probably woke up not remembering what had gone on the night before. Another sign I should have seen in my early years was my capacity to drink more than others and hold it very well. The only picture I had of an alcoholic was of bums on skid row, passed out on the street with their wine in brown paper bags. They were downtown in all big cities.

By the time I met and married Chuck, I was pretty well into my disease. I remember in the early part of our marriage when I suggested to him that we go to a bar for a few drinks, his reply was *"Why would you want to hang out in a bar? They're just islands of lonely people."* What a shock - I loved being in a bar with "my people." I had an inkling I was in trouble.

During this time I was still working at the L.A. airport. When Christmas came that year, I invited all my co-workers who were upstairs in Mike Lyman's airport bar to come home with me to continue our party. We were all pretty loaded. Chuck was in bed, and had just come off a trip. He did not think it a fun idea at all, and threw them all out and told me to go to bed. I was furious. How dare he embarrass me like that? But he did.

The first year of our marriage I was pregnant, but worked at the airport until about a month before I was scheduled to deliver. At that time I had planned to continue working after giving birth.

However, one look at my new baby girl convinced me that I could never allow anyone but myself to care for her. No doubt my ego got in my way.

It would have been healthier for me to return to work. We named her Charlene, a combination of Charles and Helen. We were both overjoyed to have such a gift. This curtailed my use of alcohol; I was into a brand new lifestyle and loving every minute of it. No more working at the airport, just being a housewife and mother, married to an airline pilot. How much better could I have had it?

A little better, apparently. I slowly got back into drinking. I hid it from my husband, tried to control the amount I consumed, and tried to cover up my indulgences with home cooking, a clean apartment, and being a good mother and wife. Sounds a little like my mother.

Eventually we were able to buy a tract house in Lawndale, not too far from the airport. By then, we were two years into the marriage and I turned up pregnant with our second child, Gloria. While pregnant, I always managed to cut way back on my consumption of alcohol, but after delivery it would start up again, still mostly hidden.

—   —   —

When I drank around my husband I tried desperately to hold back. I remember he used to be confused about how drunk I would get on two martinis. What he didn't realize was that I was sipping vodka from hidden bottles. I hid bottles in every place I thought he wouldn't find them – in the linen closet under towels, in my Kotex box, under the mattress. You name it, I stashed liquor in it.

The horrendous day came when I returned from the market and all my hidden stash was on the kitchen table. Crap! Then I knew that he knew, and the game was over. At least for that day. All that did was make me even more clever at hiding. I resorted to the trash can, the basket of dirty laundry, in the back of the freezer, etc.

Those years were spent with me trying to control my drinking, keep sober enough to take care of the two baby girls and put up a respectable front for the world to see. Believe it or not, we had a lot of great times. We went to the beach, had picnics, and shared family dinners with his family. I, of course, continued to outdo myself in the kitchen to garner praise from all about what a great cook I was.

From the outside looking in, all seemed fine. From the inside looking out, I was becoming more and more defensive and dismissive of my having a disease. I honestly thought my main problem was being married to a dud, a square who took life too seriously. I should have married a *real* military man, one who knew how to party and what fun it was.

In 1954 we were able to move to a higher-priced tract home in the Hollywood Riviera. We purchased an ocean view home that for us was sheer luxury. We even had two bathrooms! Due to the fact that all of our neighbors moved in around the same time, we had a lot in common. We were all fairly young, with little children. While there, we made good friends. We had a lot of parties and activities for the children.

My closest friend was my next-door neighbor, Ann. She was an artist, did beautiful paintings and was multi-talented. Her husband Ted was a PR man, had gone to college with Art Buchwald, and, like Art, had a great sense of humor. They had three children, two girls and a boy. Ann and I had a lot of good times together taking our kids to the beach, swimming pools and picnics. It should have been enough for me, but in spite of abstinence from alcohol at times, the drinking would always return.

_ _ _

During this time I got myself drunk one afternoon and actually called the Torrance police. I told them to come and get me, that I was a terrible mother and needed to be locked up. They were very accommodating and did just that. They arrived with a lady from the police department, took me off to jail, put me in a cell and waited for my husband to get in from his trip to come get me out. Ann took the kids.

Later that year I started drinking on my birthday, December 20th, and continued through into the new year. I can remember thinking everyone else had returned to normal living and here I was, still playing around with the bottle. It was then I called Ann and cried for help. She happened to have a brother in San Diego who had found sobriety through a well-known self-help program. I called them, and a charming woman, Marge, came over and took me to my first meeting. This was January 5th, 1955.

_ _ _

In the beginning, all went well. I couldn't believe I was not drinking, and did not want to. This lasted for about seven months, until I picked up a drink, but this time it was going to be different. I would control it! Someone had warned *"Look out for the seventh month - that's the hard one."* Boy, did I grab onto that concept and use it as an excuse. The next three years I managed to stay clean for seven months, then would have what we call relapses.

Life went on, and mostly it was good. After one of my periods of drinking again, would you believe I actually convinced my husband that my real problem was that I was an ocean person, and that if I lived right on the beach, it would be my salvation? I was a creature of the sea. The poor soul bought the idea; I always say he was ready to go to any length to help me stop drinking, years before I was ready to stop.

We sold our house and moved to a rental duplex on the Strand in Hermosa Beach. How I loved that lifestyle; the kids could play right out front and even go on the beach. The life guards there told me they would keep an eye on them for me, so I never had to worry about them.

Once again, though, it was not enough for me. However, I did get pregnant with my third girl, and that condition had always helped me to stay away from the drinking. At least I had sense enough to know that if I drank, the baby would also take in the alcohol. I think at this time I secretly believed that if I had enough children to take care of, it would solve my drinking problem.

—      —      —

Patricia was born on Mothers' Day in May of 1958. By this time I think Chuck was more in tune with the wonders of new babies, and he really pitched in and helped take care of her. He loved giving her baths, feeding her and even changing her diapers. He had made a bet with our obstetrician, double or nothing. If it was a boy, he would pay double, if a girl, she was free. That just might have had something to do with his enthusiasm. The Scotch part of him surfaced in strange ways.

Chuck was notorious for pinching a penny while enjoying spending lavishly on things like cars, airplanes, homes. It would drive him bonkers if we left a room and didn't turn off a light. He was known to drive across town for gasoline for his car if it was a few cents cheaper. I could go on and on, but you get the picture. An interesting dichotomy.

The duplex on the strand we were living in was put up for sale in 1959, but we couldn't afford to buy it. As I recall, they wanted about $39,000 for it. Today it would go for way over a million dollars. We found a rental house back up in the Hollywood Riviera and moved there.

It was during this period that I went back to the drinking with flying colors. It was so bad I began to have hallucinations and got totally out of control. By now Chuck was so frustrated and disgusted he decided to transfer to Denver, take the kids, and just walk away from me.

—      —      —

I can still recall the day when the movers came and packed all the furniture. The girls were at Chuck's mother's house and in he came. I was sitting on the floor in a corner, totally devastated. I pleaded with him to forgive me and take me with him. I promised I would never ever take another drink, no matter what. One more time, he believed me and gave in. He put me in the car to go pick up the girls, and away we went to Denver.

## *"Behind the alcohol is the woman I love."*

At this point, I am going to pause and try to tell you what was going on in my sick mind. I am sure that if there is a Heaven and I face my creator, his first question will be, *"WHAT were you THINKING?"*

I can only say that addiction is a mysterious and complex condition. There have been volumes written about it and all sorts of ideas presented regarding its origin, various forms, and treatment. I can only share what my feelings and thoughts are about it.

My personal experience with it seems to have come from masking my low self-esteem and hiding those feelings with an outer facade. When I discovered the use of alcohol, it made me feel as good as, maybe even better than others. Chuck used to be amazed at my attitude when confronted about my drinking. I was rarely on the defense, always on the offense. I'd say things like *"look at what you've done to me!"* and *"It's your fault - you're never here!"*

‒ ‒ ‒

My early drinking was to feel good, free, and able to have fun. As the years went by and the disease progressed, it evolved into escape from reality. It was all too painful to live with. My guilt, anger, fear, and resentments had to be numbed with the magic potion. I see-sawed back and forth, between escaping through drink and then over-compensating to quiet my guilt when not drinking. I was completely powerless over the choice to drink or not to drink. I was convinced it was a hopeless state for me.

Whenever I returned to the self-help program, I felt I didn't belong there. I felt like I was in an isolation booth. Those people were different, they did not understand me. They could stop drinking and live somewhat normal lives. I could not. They said I had to surrender, be willing, and be honest with myself. I think one of my stumbling blocks was learning how to be honest with myself. However, I kept going back. I had to. Praying did not work; I even asked others to pray for me and that did not work. What I would ask is, *"Please make me stop drinking. Help me to stop."* In other words, do it for me. I can't.

Now to get to the children. They never knew when the other shoe would drop. Mother was either into one of her "spells" or being the perfect, loving, over-indulgent parent. Like a yo-yo, there was no consistency in their young lives. When it was good, it was very, very good, and when it was bad, it was awful. It affected them and it affected my spouse.

Chuck tried very hard to make me stop drinking and became frustrated watching me slowly destroy myself. I know it broke his heart. He used to try to tell me, *"Behind the alcohol is the woman I love."* I didn't get it. Didn't he know that the alcohol was the woman he married? Didn't he see that if it weren't for him, his mother (who was actually wonderful and never interfered), the dogs, the kids, and on and on, that I would be OKAY?

How could I make him understand that I had to drink in order to survive? As I say, addiction is a deadly, terminal disease that destroys not only the addicted person but all those surrounding her who care.

## Denver – the Mile-High City

Denver is known as the nose-picking capital of the world. It is so high and dry that it takes time to adjust to it. The kids had nosebleeds at first but slowly became accustomed to the different climate. Coming from living in Philadelphia, New Jersey, and the short time in Wisconsin for my Navy training, I was amazed at how fast the snow melted. It was a fairyland. The summers, though short, had nights when the air felt like velvet. Our move to Denver went quite well. I was able to be a productive, loving wife and mother for almost a year. We had great family trips up to the mountains, and the children loved playing in the snow. We spent a lot of time outdoors. We had a good spell of normalcy, made friends, and were a happy family. We wanted to live out of the city in a more rural setting, so we moved from our house out to Broomfield, which is between Denver and Boulder.

–      –      –

Then it all came back. It was the one thing Chuck could never understand - how, knowing what I knew by then, and when all was going so well, I could pick up a drink and start again.

I have heard a theory about that, that we alcoholics, while still in the disease, cannot deal with the responsibilities involved when we have to face the stress of normal living. Whatever it was, I kept going back to the bottle.

At one point I even figured if the program for recovery worked so well, and I had seen that it did, I could use it to drink. I took the Serenity Prayer and each day used it in this way:

*God grant me the serenity to accept the things I cannot change* (I am an
   alcoholic and I can't change that),
*The courage to change the things I can* (the amount of alcohol I consume
   today),
*And the wisdom to know the difference* (I ignored that).


What a crock! It worked for a few months, and I was ready to write a
new book for the alcoholic. We just needed to find our level of consumption
and we could drink successfully.

During this period I drank a pint of brandy and a six-pack of king-size cans
of beer a day. I drank the beer during the day and saved the brandy for
after the kids went to bed. In about three months that level just wasn't enough,
and away I went. I have no idea why I felt the need to drink even more.

One more time a beautiful woman from "the program" came when I
called for help. Her name was Wibbie and she was such fun, so vivacious,
so loving. Wibbie stayed by my side, literally, for the next two years. I even
made a whole year sober up there. I used to kid around and say it must be
the altitude. It caught up with me after the year, however. This time it
involved a suicide attempt and ending up in a psychiatric unit. Can you see
the progression?

After recovery from that episode, I turned up pregnant with my fourth
child, our first boy, Charles. We were so pleased. By now I was 41 years
old. I did not pick up a drink during this pregnancy, thank God! In hind-
sight, at my age I should have gone into Denver for care during this pregnancy. Instead I opted to go to Boulder, which was closer and had less traffic. There I had a young doctor without much experience.

At the end of the nine months, we found the baby was in a breach position. How the doctor handled that was to dose me with castor oil to force
the delivery, and try to turn the baby manually. When I went into labor it
was chaotic. Charles started to come out feet first, in the labor room. They
wheeled me into the delivery room, and with no anesthesia forced the child
from my womb. I'm sure today they would perform a caesarean delivery,
but in 1961 it just was not done unless they thought it was an emergency.

After five or six months, it was obvious Charles had a problem; he could
not sit up, and we had problems with feeding. All babies are spastic and
athetoid with random movements, so that did not concern us, but we finally
found a pediatric neurologist who gave us the correct diagnosis. We were
told that Charles had Cerebral Palsy.

We were told it was brain damage that had occurred during birth, similar to a stroke later in life. How much damage is done and which part of the brain is affected determines the amount of disability the child has. Fortunately his intellect was not affected, but no one knew how long it would be before he could walk.

This was a traumatic time for all of us. Once again my alcoholic mind took over and I was sure I was to blame. My anger at God and life was intense. If I was going to be punished, why wasn't I crippled? What was fair about doing this to our baby? At one point I went into a rage and broke furniture, tore drapes off the windows, and tried to destroy everything in our house. That did nothing to alter the situation. Somehow, some way, we had to do whatever we could for our boy, and that became our focal point.

We were told that Los Angeles had the best care facilities. We were referred to a doctor at the University of Southern California who was doing physical therapy on these children with some success. We decided we had no choice but to relocate back to the Los Angeles area. Chuck was magnificent and gave all the time and care he possibly could to Charlie.

Our girls had to go along with whatever was decided needed to be done to help Charles, and it changed the way we could travel and what our outdoor activities could be. We put a swimming pool in our back yard so they could keep active and have friends over. It was wonderful how they accepted this curtailment and found other activities and friends to keep them busy.

We found a new tract home on the eastern side of the Palos Verdes Peninsula. This was the area we had always dreamed of being able to afford to live in. It was adjacent to the Pacific Ocean, convenient to the freeways, and yet more rural than most areas in Los Angeles.

We located Dr. Rood at USC, and she accepted Charles for the class in which she taught her methods to therapists. I was able to observe the classes, and could continue the therapy at home. It consisted of using ice on his legs and back, and an electric brush to stimulate the nerves and muscles.

In those days there was no central place you could go for advice and help. As parents you just had to be diligent and do a lot of research. After a lot of research, and a new evaluation at UCLA Medical Center, we located a preschool in Long Beach for children wih Cerebral Palsy. It had the best therapy and care available. Charles was enrolled at the tender age of 18 months.

A magnificent woman named Hazel Olds ran the school. She did a fantastic job, and we will be forever grateful to her for the work she did. The first time I visited the school, I had a feeling come over me that they were all little angels, on loan to us from Heaven. They were all so beautiful and loving.

Miss Olds taught Charles to swim under water, and after that we thought he'd never swim on top; he was just like a little frog. She helped him to stop grinding his teeth and stop drooling, to be comfortable in a social setting, and started him on reading and writing. He attended that school until the age of 3, then transferred to Harlan Shoemaker in San Pedro, a school for the handicapped (that was the term used back then).

During these years Charles had several surgical procedures on his legs to help him walk. The emotional pain we went through is indescribable. To have been on the other side of the crib and watch his tortured body twitch and turn in pain is more than I can relate. One doctor stood by us and said, *"Know that your pain is greater than what he is feeling."* He was nice to try and make us feel better, but I didn't believe him for a second.

## Japan

Early in March of 1964, Chuck came home from a trip with the news that he could get a leave of absence from the airline if he was willing to go to Japan for six months to train Japan Airline (JAL) pilots in the DC-6 (a somewhat new Douglas commercial airplane). He asked me and our children how we felt about living over there for that period of time.
Charlene was 13, Gloria 11, Patricia 6, and Charles 3. The older girls were all for it and so was I. It sounded like a great adventure, a way for me personally to escape from my routine. We checked with all the schools they were attending and got the response that it would be an excellent educational experience. So Chuck volunteered to go, we packed, leased our house for the six months we'd be gone, and off we went.

—    —    —

We flew on JAL and had a memorable trip. It seemed like they did nothing but feed us from Los Angeles to Tokyo. We stopped in Hawaii for re-fueling. This was my first trip to that paradise. On approach they played Hawaiian music over the loud speakers, and when the pilot cut back the engines it felt as though we were floating in space. The sky was blue, the clouds pure white, and this island appearing in the vast expanse of the Pacific was enchanting. It was as close to my idea of Heaven as was possible.

Back then the Royal Hawaiian Hotel was prominent on the shoreline. What a sight, like a pink jewel adorning the beach! Today, it is almost hid-

120

den among the sprawling high-rise hotels and condominiums that surround it. We deplaned in Hawaii and I learned immediately that one does not wear a black wool suit in Hawaii. Wow, was I ever uncomfortable!

We were soon back on the plane. During this part of the trip the pilot introduced himself to us, and offered to help in any way he could. His name was Ryan and he had flown for several years for JAL, so he knew the country quite well. He lived in a small seaside town, Hayama, thirty miles south of Tokyo. It was also the location of the Emperor's Summer Palace.

We arrived in Tokyo in the late evening, during a heavy rain. Surprisingly, a representative of the airline was there to greet us. It seemed to us to be routine, but later he told us he just had to see and meet a pilot who was bringing his wife and four kids to a new country. Most of the other pilots recruited for this purpose came alone. A few who did bring wives had to send them back to the States. They were unable to adjust to the lifestyle. So there we were!

—   —   —

I called it the land of the "open fly." It was acceptable back then for the men to urinate in public. Anywhere, any time. I guess things like that, along with the smells and strange (to us) foods, not to mention the population density, were just too much for some Americans to deal with. I found it intriguing to experience a new country and new customs. I was a visitor, it was their country and their lifestyle, and it was up to me to adjust.

After the customs ordeal, we were taken to a hotel near the airport. Dan, the JAL delegate, came with us to make sure we got settled in. My memory of that evening is of total exhaustion. We were dealing with getting the kids tucked in while Dan went on and on about the country, its traditions and culture, not to mention the language and the exchange rate for yen. In the condition we were in, neither of us was able to comprehend any of it.

We stayed at the hotel for at least two weeks. During that time, Chuck reported for duty and was given two weeks to settle in. We started the search for a rental house. The staff at the hotel were very gracious and took over watching the children while we were gone. After about one day with a rental agent in Tokyo, I knew we had to find something out of the city. Everywhere we went there were crowds of people and unbelievable traffic. It was quite overwhelming.

We called Ryan, the pilot we had met earlier, and he suggested we come down to Hayama and look around. He referred us to an agent he knew, Reiko Ichikawa. The transportation system was phenomenal, and navigable even by newcomers like us. Trains and buses enabled us to go anywhere in the area. We took off for Hayama to meet with Reiko.

Our new friend was a most unusual female in that ancient civilization. Once, after imbibing sufficient sake, she confided to me that she had learned her perfect English in bed from GIs after the war. Oh, she did like the men!

Reiko was a shrewd businesswoman; she had a real estate business, shares in the telephone company, and owned many rental properties. Luckily for us, she had a brand-new corner house across the bay that was vacant.

It was a typical Japanese house, with tatami mat floors and rooms separated by sliding shoji screens. The outside walls were a combination of sliding screens and wooden sliding doors, for protection against typhoons and cold. The downstairs had a large living space, kitchen, and separate bath area.

The toilet and shower were separated by a wall, and there was a hot-tub adjacent to the shower. The hot-tub had an individual heater for the water, to be lit for the bathing time and turned off afterwards. The procedure was to take a shower first, then soak in the tub. The man, of course, was first, followed by the wife and children. One time, Chuck fell asleep in the tub with the heater lit and came out looking like a lobster, screaming, *"Why didn't you wake me?"* We hadn't noticed he was in there.

There was also a small bathroom in the hall right as you entered the house, with a urinal and a toilet on the floor. I found that to be quite a challenge to use. The locals just squatted with ease, but not so for this Western woman. I lost my balance once and knocked off the tank lid, breaking it to smithereens.

The second floor had two bedrooms, separated with shoji screens. We slept on the floor on futons, and rolled them up during the day. We had a small bathroom upstairs with a real flushing American toilet. It had a small sticker on the bowl with stick figures showing them how to use it – male standing, woman sitting. (I still have it, framed and in my guest bath.)

We were located on a main corner in town, very convenient to the bus stop. Most of the streets were so narrow that it amazed me to be on a bus that was passing another vehicle on the street and not have the paint scraped off on the sides. Talk about close! Due to the population density, many people wore masks as protection from getting germs or spreading them.

Houses and stores were constructed of wood siding, some with green tile roofs. They actually swept and watered the dirt out front to keep it as clean as possible. Hayama was damp, situated on Sagami Bay and having heavy rainfall averages. We had to keep our shoes and clothes in tea boxes lined with foil, to protect them from the dampness and mold. On the side streets and alleys I traveled to shop there were many rock walls, covered with moss. It felt like an old, old country, steeped in their culture and traditions.

–      –      –

I cooked for a family of six on a two-burner propane stove. It took quite a bit of juggling and I got very creative. I even bought an oven that fit over a burner, and learned to bake cakes and pies, a very tricky process.

When I went shopping for food I resorted to charades to make my wants known, such as flapping my arms for chicken wings or pointing to my breast for white meat. A trip to the fish market meant making motions to remove head and tail and asking, *"Dijob tempura?,"* hoping it meant *"Is it OK for frying?"* They answered, *"Hai"* (yes) for everything, so I was never quite sure.

Vegetables were relatively easy, but did need to be washed thoroughly in a special soap. Back in those days they still used human waste for fertilizer. I will say that they were the best tasting veggies and fruit I have ever eaten. We were fortunate enough to have had a small ice box shipped over. Most of the locals did not have refrigeration, and shopped daily for their food supply. There was always a steady stream of Mama-sans shuffling by on their way to and from the local stores.

The one thing I finally learned was that there was no way you could get one-up on the Japanese as far as gifts are concerned. They would leave gifts of special foods, holiday rice dishes, and treats (some we couldn't identify) by our back or side door. I would return with home-made cake or pie and back would come another gift. I never did get even!

They loved giving small gifts lavishly wrapped in silk scarves. This was for any occasion, dropping by for a visit, any holiday. They were big on holidays – children's day, old folks' day, start of summer, end of summer, Emperor's birthday. You name it, they celebrated it.

–      –      –

Speaking of the start of summer, we arrived in April and moved to Hayama to get away from Tokyo. By the end of June we discovered that what seemed like most of Tokyo came to Hayama for the summer. We were on the busiest corner in town, and literally could not leave the house on weekends. Multitudes of humans, buses, and cars, all outside our front gate.

We got our beach time in during the week, and even then it was mobbed. It was still fun, though. They had rows of shacks lined up selling all sorts of sushi, saimen, ramen, and, once again, who knew what?

The children all went to different schools. Fortunately we were allowed to send them to the English-speaking military schools in Yokahama. This was a 20-mile school bus ride from Hayama.

Reiko took us on interesting trips. Once we went fishing on Sagami Bay. That was quite an adventure. We were on a good-sized boat with a neat glass-bottomed middle section for holding the fish we caught. We dropped lines over the side with about four or five clumps of chum which looked like spaghetti, and almost immediately we would hook as many fish.

The toilet for women was a bucket behind a partial screen, and there you were, in front of God and all on board, exposed from the waist up, trying to look cool while urinating. The men, of course, just aimed over the rail.

We brought in a huge haul of who knows what kind of fish, and gave it to our Papa San next door. He made a huge vat of fish stew that everyone in the neighborhood seemed to enjoy. The fish heads in it turned us off, though. The Japanese did seem to love their fish heads.

Charles and I were taken by Reiko on an all-day trip to a Japanese Inn, where her husband was staying for a few days of rest and play. The girls were all in school, and I had a housekeeper to take care of them when they returned. On arrival, the staff was lined up at the entrance to greet us. They immediately took Charles from me to carry (he was not walking yet). We were ushered through many hallways, past game rooms alive with Pachinko machines (their version of slots), restaurants, and a pool. Very posh.

Our destination was a large room where several men came and went all afternoon. There was lots of food and drink available. Naturally, I had no idea of what was going on, but was practically forced to take a hot bath in mineral water, and decided to take Charles in with me. It was hot, and soon Reiko had her blouse off and was sitting on the floor playing a card game with some of the men. None of our puritanical hang-ups.

The remarkable thing I remember about that day is that all the men were quite intoxicated and noisy until about 4 p.m. At that time they disappeared one by one, and in about one hour re-appeared; they were sober, meticulously dressed in business suits, and ready to return to the real world. Amazing! What control and self-discipline they had.

—     —     —

Our son Charles was completely taken in by our next door neighbors, who had some sort of a food shop. They adored and worshiped him. He would be propped up at their family table and played with and fed all day. He got to know more of the language than any of us. Problem was, none of us knew what he was saying.

We did experience a *simultaneous* typhoon and earthquake while there.

Naturally, Chuck was gone on a trip (he often was during an emergency). My neighbors swarmed around our house, closing all the wooden shutters. I had no idea we were in for a typhoon. That night was a scary one. Our house rattled and shook, the wind howled, and we had a deluge of rain. The children and I snuggled together upstairs on our futons. The next day we heard that in addition to the typhoon, there had been five earthquakes. Another major problem in Japan is the landslides caused by such heavy rains.

—      —      —

We were in Japan for six months. Can you imagine all television programs, including our cartoons, with not a word of English? Naturally, there were no English newspapers or magazines locally. Toward the end of our stay Chuck and I resorted to reading the Palos Verdes phone book to each other, to see how many people we knew.

One of the fun things I did was to go next door to Reiko's and sit and listen to her telephone conversations. *"Moshi-moshi"* seemed to be the main way of greeting and signing off on all calls.

She was forever trying to get me to take a bath at her home. They had mineral water in their tub and seemed sure it was the one and only way to bathe. All in all, I dearly loved the opportunity and adventure to live with those gentle folk.

They adored children and spoiled them rotten. Once old enough to attend school, they were pressured to maintain excellent grades. The middle years were to be the productive ones, and the older generation were truly revered.

Most of the homes had a small shrine in the home or back yard to worship their ancestors. Honor was important. Simplicity and meditation were a must. They taught me many things to live by.

I was amazed to discover these aspects of the Japanese. During WWII, they had been depicted as cruel monsters. I agree that its military back then were truly terrible, but the majority of its citizens certainly were not. How is it that we so easily forget that we are all the same, all human beings?

## Do Not Pass Go - Go Directly to Jail

Dear God, I do not like to say what was happening to me. My periods of sobriety were becoming less frequent. By now, back in California, I was simply running away from home for several days at a time, abandoning the children. I would time my escapes to coincide with Chuck's arrival from his trips. We played games such as *"I'll run away, you come find me,"* *"Bottle, bottle, where is the bottle?,"* and *"I'll show you, I can drink if I want to!"* One of my favorite comebacks seems to have been, *"I couldn't care less."*

My escapades started to involve the law. One time I was driving in Inglewood, looking for the American Legion hall where I knew the bartender. I was in our family station wagon, and, as always, had an open bottle by me. I pulled out from a side street onto La Brea Boulevard, making a left turn that was a bit too wide. My rear right bumper hooked the left front bumper of a Volkswagen parked on the street. What a mess; I continued down the street, frantically trying to unhook the little devil, hoping no one would notice. It finally broke free and, lo and behold, there I was right in front of the Legion. It happened to be Sunday evening and the darn place was closed.

As I couldn't get in, I ran around the back and hid to see if I heard any sirens or noise. All seemed OK so I went back out to get into the car. There was a little old man by the car and he put out his arm to stop me and said, *"Don't get in it."* (To this day I think it was God.) Then I heard the police cars approaching from both directions, sirens blaring and red lights flashing. You would have thought I'd robbed a bank! Evidently someone did notice my condition. I did not pass "Go", and went directly to jail.

There were several other instances when I got caught short and visited the local jail. One time in Santa Ana when I was lost and trying to find Theda's house, I sped out of a gas station where I was trying to get directions and hit a Cadillac. And on it went.

The saddest part of these episodes is that I could always talk Chuck into covering for me. He would bail me out, go to court for me, and pay whatever fines were involved. I never really had to face the consequences of my actions. What a con artist I had become.

How Chuck could deal with all of this and still maintain his sense of humor is a mystery to me. One time I stated if I ever picked up another drink, I would go straight to skid row. I did pick one up and went straight to Santa Monica, where I had bartender friends and knew the territory.

Chuck came home and did the usual chase scene, but this time went downtown to skid row. He said as soon as he got there he realized I would never actually go there. While stalking the area he got a ticket for jaywalking. After his anger died down he thought it pretty funny that I came home clean and he had to pay a ticket.

One Sunday morning when I was on the couch, nursing the usual hangover, he was reading the paper and ignoring the half-dead body in the room. All of a sudden I reared up and said, *"I bet you think I am pretty dumb and stupid, don't you?"* He grunted in return. I said *"Well, I do know one thing - I can tell you the price of every used car on the market!"*

At this time I spent many a night with the TV on all night, watching all the used-car salesmen pitching their wares. Although in a fairly comatose state, I still absorbed some of it. He said, *"The hell you can,"* turned to the car ads, and quizzed me on pricing. I was right on every one of them and I tell you, he was impressed!

—       —       —

Chuck was what is referred to in the world of addiction as a flaming co-dependent, and was he ever! At times he would almost reward me for a drinking spell. When I returned to sobriety, I would be dined, just not wined!

Life for me was a nightmare. I totally lost control and knew it. I went from a psychiatric unit to a recovery home for women in Long Beach, the House of Hope. Not one thing was working for me - I was hopeless. I actually got to a place where the thought of sobriety was worse than staying the way I was. It was more familiar and safer for me to continue to try to control the drinking; with any luck I might even die. That would relieve the family of all the agony I was putting them through, and they could perhaps begin to live a somewhat normal life.

—       —       —

Those who had tried to help me so many times before stopped coming around. Our social life had simply died. We were in a downward spiral, and misery reigned in our home. It was then that Chuck offered me a deal. He said that he knew I had tried to stop drinking and could not do it. He also stated that he could not leave me or throw me out, that I was his wife and the mother of our children, and that he knew I loved them and him. His proposition was that he would supply me with my necessary "medicine," but I could no longer drive the car. The deal was for me to try to do the best I could and the family would do their best. He also stated he and the children would try to live "around " me.

This was good and bad. Yes, I had my precious alcohol, but I was completely cut off from not only the outside world, but my own family in my home. It took about three months of our new program for me to finally see that my major problem was *my* decision to put drink to my lips and consume it. Not one person, place, or thing had a thing to do with it; it was strictly my doing. For the first time, I also became aware that my drinking was destroying the whole family and anyone who cared about me.

## Surrender

On June 4th, 1967, I got up with my usual hangover, went to the kitchen, and sat on a bar stool at the counter. Our telephone was right there and in my mind came the memory of the first woman who had called on me, saying, *"You have to believe in a Higher Power."*

It can be anything, just as long as you believe. Looking at the phone, I knew if I used it I could once more get help; it was a connection, it was a power. How it worked was a mystery. I asked that phone to please, *"Give me the courage to change."* It was the first time I prayed for me to have the strength; before then it was always to make me stop or help me to stop.

—     —     —

Chuck came in from the garage just then and said, *"You look like Hell. I'll go down and get you some beer."* For the first time in many a year I heard myself say *"No thanks, I do not want to drink!"* Unbelievable, but I meant every word.

If it took being chained to my bed with a 24-hour guard to stop me if the compulsion returned, that would be OK. If they wanted to tattoo "alcoholic" on my forehead, fine. At last I was willing to do whatever it took to not pick up a drink.

What happened that morning was that I had at long last surrendered my will and my life to a power outside of myself. I did what they had been trying to share with me for twelve and a half years, what was necessary for me to do to get sober and stay sober, one day at a time. The miracle happened!

—     —     —

An interesting aspect of my experience in the world of addiction that Sobriety made me aware of was the total reversal of my choice of color, surroundings, and environment. During the last years of my drinking, I wanted black furniture and heavy drapes; a total closed-in feeling. It reflected the way I felt about life. My living room, which I had personally decorated, consisted of deep green and gold shag carpet, a dark gold couch, dark brown and tan grass wall paper, and a beaded curtain at the doorway. It ended up looking like an opium den. After my surrender, what I wanted was bright color and open windows. I wanted to be back in the real world, after so long spent trying to escape from it.

—     —     —

The family took a long time getting around to believing this was it. How many times had they heard my promise to never drink again? How many times did they hear, *"This time it will be different"*? How many times had I convinced my husband to let me try to control my drinking?

What was necessary for me was to stay close to my support group, and to try to get an understanding of the need for me to change just about everything about myself. My way surely hadn't worked; in fact, it had almost completely destroyed me and my family. Thus I began my journey into a life clean and sober. And what a difference it made.

I became president of the parents' group at Harlan Shoemaker, which my son Charles still attended. My activities included the "self-help program," and Las Esperanzas, a support group for the House of Hope in Long Beach. The House of Hope was a recovery home for women, the same one I had been incarcerated in many times before.

—    —    —

In other words, I slowly assumed the responsibilities involved in being a wife and mother. The rewards were beyond belief. Our lives changed dramatically. Charlene was now 16, Gloria 14, and both were in high school. Patricia was 9 and Charles was 6. They were all involved in the usual school activities. Chuck was busy with the airline, and had become Safety Chairman.

We were making new friends and joined in airline functions, neighborhood activities, and school affairs. I became more and more involved with my program for recovery and its offshoots. It was as if the sun had come out; it was daytime and we were alive.

## Life after Recovery

Gradually my family became more confident that this time was for real. Time passed, Charlene graduated from high school and decided to attend junior college in San Luis Obispo. Then Gloria graduated. Patricia was about to enter high school, and Charles had been what they referred to as "mainstreamed," and enrolled in elementary school in Palos Verdes.

Chuck had always hung around the small airports when he had days off. I used to say he was an airplane with legs. Over the years I tried convincing him to take up golf or tennis, but his true and only love was flying.

We went through a period of boating. He purchased a 33-foot Owens twin-engine boat. It was fun for us, but also quite a drag to spend a day or two getting ready, go over to Catalina Island for a night or two, and then have to spend two days unpacking and cleaning the boat to put it back at the dock. We ran out of enthusiasm in about a year and sold it.

One day Chuck took me for a ride to the Compton airport, got out, and suggested that we go up to the observation deck and watch the airplanes. When we got up there he pointed down below to a row of SNJs and asked me if I would like it if we had one of those. To his complete surprise, I was delighted and said I sure would!

It happened to be the same type of airplane I had first flown in during the war, down in Corpus Christi, when the Chief had taken me with him on the mail run to the outlying bases. We bought one, and flying in it gave me a feeling of total freedom. It felt like my sobriety; I could feel, see and experience life. It was thrilling and magnificent, cruising along at about 325 mph.

The next several years we had a marvelous time going to air shows, fly-ins, and lots of times just to Catalina or some small airport for lunch or breakfast. Chuck was in heaven, his dream come true, his own airplane just for play. Big boys need big toys.

—         —         —

It was in 1972 that Chuck bought me a new gold Cadillac for Mother's Day. He told me it was because I was solid gold now. We went on trips by car or plane to visit Charlene in San Luis Obispo, where she was attending college. We landed at a small airport in Oceano, near the beach. I loved the area so very much that I convinced Chuck we needed to buy a beach house there for our vacations and visits.

We met a local couple named Linda and Harry who sold real estate, and through them we bought two beach lots and built two A-frame houses. We sold one and used the other. They also had the flying bug, and we became close friends and would meet up at air shows and fly-ins.

By now we'd decided we wanted to live in the country, and once more we uprooted and moved, this time to Arroyo Grande, inland a bit from Oceano. We purchased a huge ranch home. It had six bedrooms, and we used them all.

Daughter Gloria had become pregnant in high school, married the guy, then immediately divorced him. She gave us our beautiful granddaughter Shannon. Soon the two of them moved in, joining Patricia and Charles.

My nephew Jimmy, my brother Jim's son, had been in the Navy on Terminal Island near us. He spent much of his free time at our home, and when we went to Arroyo Grande, he moved in, too! He was like another son. Charlene would come and visit from school. It was great fun, and we had good times living in that area. We spent a lot of time at the beach and took trips exploring central California.

Chuck bought another small airplane and commuted to San Francisco for

Chuck and I in our SNJ trainer over Palm Springs, California.

his flights with the airline. This got difficult at times when the weather turned bad, but he made it work.

After about a year, Jimmy left to go back to New Jersey to his parents. Gloria had connected with a great guy who was attending college, and she moved in with him. She and Lance eventually married, and he became a doting father to Shannon.

Charles and Patricia were not too happy with the schools there and I got homesick for Palos Verdes and old friends. I think by then Chuck was tired of commuting, so back to Palos Verdes we went, lock, stock, and barrel.

We found a fantastic house in Palos Verdes, in the area called Rolling Hills Estates. It was a perfect location and had a swimming pool and horse facilities. We had two black Labradors and used the horse area to build dog runs for them. Charles and Patricia were doing well in school and made good friends. We were home, and it all just felt right.

Chuck started ferrying old World War II airplanes for a museum out in Chino, and was kept busy by the airline and our own SNJ. Life was good. We both had busy social lives, and had many great parties in our home. It was such fun to throw parties that didn't revolve around alcohol. Due to my activities with recovery, I had made countless true friends.

—     —     —

One in particular was Sue. She was married to an airline pilot, and was also in the program, so we had a lot in common. Sue was more fun to be with than any other human being I have encountered. I honestly believe she had a tape of jokes in her head that was unending. Unfortunately, she was also manic-depressive. This made her more fun than the proverbial pack of monkeys when she was in her "up" cycle, but when the depression hit, she would isolate herself, write morose letters, not sleep, and in general suffer.

Sue and I were like Laurel and Hardy, always ending up with one or the other of us saying, *"Another fine mess you got me in, Ollie!"* For example, once we decided it would be keen to go out to the Hemet area and go up in a hot air balloon. We took son Charles with us for the adventure, who at the time was in a leg cast following surgery.

Several balloons were gathered in an open field. The deal was to go for the ride, then on landing to have champagne and breakfast. The pilot helped us enter the basket under the balloon, and then we stood upright for the ride. The ground crew untied the ropes holding the balloon on the ground, the flame was turned on, and up we went.

It was a beautiful Sunday morning, and in between the blasts firing to keep the thing in the air, it was silent and magical. We just seemed to float above the countryside.

All went well until the wind started to come up. The pilot indicated he would have to land, and we started to descend. He tried to land in an open space beside a horse corral, but a farmer came out with a shotgun, shouting at us to go away, saying we were scaring the horses. We then went back up a bit, over to a field that had been stripped of whatever crop it had yielded. Down we went. The wind caught the balloon as we hit the ground, and we tipped over and were bounced roughly across the deeply furrowed field.

When the basket tipped over, the pilot and Charles ended up on the bottom, with Sue and me piled on top of them. The two of us got to laughing so hard that we wet not only ourselves, but showered them as well.

Although glad to be down safely, we were in no mood to celebrate. The thought of breakfast was not appealing, and we couldn't drink the champagne anyway. We were battered and bruised, not to mention a little damp, so we got in our car and went home. Another fine mess she got me in!

One time Sue and I were trying to figure out why our husbands stayed with us through our years of alcoholism. We reached the conclusion that it had to have been due to the fact that we were so good in bed. Later when the four of us were out to dinner, the subject somehow came up and, we told them about our reasoning. Chuck looked at me askance and said, *"Whatever made you think that? You either smelled so bad I couldn't get near you, or you would pass out in the 'middle' of."* There went another illusion.

I dearly loved Sue and I still miss her daily. She passed away when I lived in Hawaii. One of the most difficult things I have had to do was give her eulogy. I depended on my higher power to help me with that one and it worked.

—  —  —

Due to all my experience in the field of alcoholism, in 1975 I was hired as a counselor in a program at a Long Beach hospital. In those days, we qualified for this work without degrees, etc., using what they called "grandfather" knowledge. This, in addition to all my other activities, really kept me hopping. My natural philosophy in life has always been if a little bit is good, more is better. Of course, that same philosophy had also led to my downfall.

How I did enjoy this type of work. I felt I was really giving back what had been so freely given me. The unconditional love both given and received was more than I can describe. To watch seemingly hopeless and helpless humans get the message, to see the light come back in their eyes and the smiles return to their faces is a privilege I do not take lightly. I am grateful each and every day of my life.

Reflecting on these years, I also realize I was away from the family much too much. I got so deeply involved with me and my life that they were somewhat marginalized. They were delighted to have me vertical and happy, but I think they could have used more stability in the home. Again, all I can say is that I did the best I could, and in doing so saved my life.

## Tragedy Strikes

During the month of October, 1979, all was going well. Chuck was flying to Mexico City that month, I was working, and Charles was going to school and keeping busy. Patricia had met and married a guy from Alameda and now had a small child, Leon. Her husband turned out to be a disaster. He not only used drugs but dealt in them. After years of her leaving him and then going back, he eliminated himself by overdosing. Not a happy ending.

—       —       —

The evening of October 30th Chuck was at home, preparing to leave on his red-eye flight to Mexico City. I happened to be cooking his favorite meal, our version of macaroni and cheese and ham slices. I was also baking his favorite pound cake. He got up from a nap and came in the kitchen and was poking around. He tried to get some butter out of the batter I was putting together, and I told him hands off, it was a measured amount. His retort was, *"Hell, Helen, you never measured anything in your life!"* How right he was!

He received a phone call from a friend we flew with who raised a son alone. When he hung up he came back in the kitchen, hugged me, and said, *"You have given me everything."* This was a most unusual demonstration of love from him, and I was surprised.

After dinner, he got dressed and came into the family room, where I was watching the news. He kissed me goodbye and said *"I'll see you tomorrow night."* At that time, we had a garage door which we had to manually open and close. I told him, *"Don't bother with the garage door. I'll get it for you."* He said *"Gee, thanks,"* and then left. I mention all this because it was not really normal behavior for either of us. Was it a premonition? I'll never know.

On the morning of October 31st, 1979, I was awakened by a phone call at about 5:30 am from Chuck's friend Stan, who flew with us in our flying club at the Compton airport. I was due to go to work that morning and was annoyed by the call. I told Stan, *"Chuck isn't here. He's in Mexico City."* Stan replied, *"I know. Helen, turn on the news. I am afraid there is trouble in Mexico City."* My reply was, *"Stan, there is always trouble in Mexico City."* (They were prone to overthrow their presidents regularly back then.)

Stan insisted I get up and check the news, that a plane was down. I told Stan *"OK, but it can't be Chuck. He isn't even there yet."* I got up, turned on the TV, and heard there had been a crash in Mexico City. I knew the airline would send a representative to our house if there had been a disaster, and that hadn't happened, so I held out hope. Then I received a call from another pilot friend, who confirmed it was Chuck. Thus the nightmare began.

— — —

First I had to deal with my son Charles, who started rocking back and forth and uttering soul-wrenching, unearthly sounds. He retreated to his bedroom, and I got on the phone and started to inform family, friends, and my work of the situation. The rest of the day is a blur. Friends kept coming, the family started to appear. Even my brother and his wife arrived later in the day from Alabama. The phone rang incessantly but I was kept from it. The president of the airline called and pleaded with me to not watch the news on television.

There were early reports that perhaps the crew had survived, but they turned out to be false. The airline rep arrived but I already knew what had happened. Other pilots came and went and phoned from airports all over.

He had so many friends from the airline, the flying club, and his ferrying of aircraft for the Chino Museum; it was very moving. Everyone kept saying what a great pilot he was and how he had helped them.

The next few days turned into a three-ring circus. With so many friends and family surrounding me, all the news and media on the scene, and decisions to be made about a memorial service, it was utter chaos. Luckily for me I had near and dear friends in my life from the "program." It is hard to explain the bonding we experience with each other. The unconditional love, caring and compassion is deeper than ties between children, spouse, or others in our lives.

They came in, took over, and handled all the arrangements for me. My memory is that the crash was on a Wednesday morning and I wanted to have the memorial as soon as possible. We decided on the following Sunday. I wanted it to be more of a retirement party, just one that Chuck would not be able to attend. Because it had happened in Mexico City, we had no idea of when and if his remains would be returned. We got a call from the airline Saturday, and he was here. That meant contacting a funeral director, etc. Once again, it was handled by my support group.

Sunday we went to Green Hills for the service. There were hundreds of people there – old friends like Theda, Wibbie from Broomfield, airline employees, and, of course, the good old media. It was a fitting tribute to my loved one. His squadron of AT-6s from Compton did a missing man formation fly-by, Sue's husband Jack scattered rose petals from a small private airplane, and another pilot from Orange County did sky writing in his memory; a cross, his initials, and a heart. The amazing thing was that it was quite a windy day, yet the tribute stayed overhead for a long time. We also had the Marines there for the presentation of the flag and military salute.

After the service we all went back to the house. The women and men in my life at that time arrived with so much food that it was unbelievable. It kept coming in the back door. We had a few hundred people to feed and without supplying any of it, it just appeared. How loving and caring they were. In time of need, friends are there!

A few days later, we scattered his ashes from an AT-6 out over the ocean by Catalina. I flew with them, and it is a sight still etched in my memory. When we took off in formation, it was a cloudy day. When we arrived at the point where his friend Stan dropped the ashes, the sun broke out over Catalina island. It looked like a huge green jewel rising out of the ocean. I had a wonderful sensation that we were setting him free.

—    —    —

What followed were months of confusion. It turned out that Chuck's flight crashed on landing at the Mexico City airport. My understanding is that he was given clearance to land on a runway that had just been closed, even though he'd used it all month. That morning there were men and equipment on the runway, but the notice to airmen usually issued about this did not come out until the next day. At the last minute, coming out of morning fog, he saw the equipment on the runway and attempted to pull up and go around, but his left landing wheel hit a truck and the airplane cartwheeled and crashed into a building, caught fire and was demolished.

We will never know for sure what really went wrong. I know from living with a pilot all those years that when there is a crash, it is never just one thing involved. It is always a series of incidents that culminate in the disaster. We do know that the early morning hour is when we are at our lowest ebb. We also know that Chuck was having friction with his first officer. It seems he was having problems at home and kept showing up for flights

On our Wedding Day, March 9th, 1951    Chuck in Western Airlines pilot uniform.

Taken at the last party we attended.    Skywriting at Chuck's funeral in 1979.

137

without proper uniform. That was a big no-no for Chuck. Mexico City was also one of the lowest-rated airports for safety. Their navigation aids and methods were antiquated, to say the least.

They removed the wreckage immediately, whereas here in the U.S. we carefully examine and reconstruct the remnants to help find the cause. The air traffic controller on duty in the tower that day simply disappeared, so the whole investigation was flawed. I did read their report on the findings and they contradicted themselves several times in it.

Several months later I went to Washington to try to persuade our country to further investigate, but was told it wasn't going to happen. Seems we did not want Mexico angry with us. Diplomats, ugh! I was even told, *"Just go home and shut up,"* and *"That order came from higher up,"* whatever that meant.

At that point I personally gave up. The bottom line was that Chuck was gone. Maybe he'd made a mistake, he was human after all. What remains fixed in my mind, however, was his dedication to the airline and the safety of his passengers. He was truly a pilot's pilot.

—        —        —

The airline could not have been kinder to us. They saw to it that every expense we'd incurred during this time was covered. They offered counseling and kept in touch with me for months following the disaster.

At one point during the months following the crash, a few officials and pilots came to our home to question me regarding Chuck's activities prior to the day he left on that last flight. I was beginning to feel the full impact of his death. Tearfully, I asked them, *"Where did all his knowledge, experience and devotion to flying and the airline go?"* Their reply was, *"It is encompassed in the lives of all the men he flew with."* I think a quote from John Quincy Adams also gives us an answer: *"The influence of each human being on others in this life is a kind of immortality."*

## The Dark Side...Chuck

And so, we come to yet another awakening. I was well aware that Chuck had his share of problems. As a young boy he witnessed his father and uncles drinking to excess, and the behavior that went along with it. His mother was a passive, soft woman who had also undergone trauma as a child. Seems to me we just keep inheriting some of this stuff and passing it on to our children. Especially in the past, when counseling and support groups were non-existent. I'm not trying to make excuses; that's just the way it was, or at least the way I see it as having been. His father was anything but faithful, and was also known to get physically abusive while under the influence.

During the years of our marriage when I was into the escaping and binge-drinking, there were times when there was limited physical abuse. In all fairness to Chuck, though, I have to say I really goaded him, and also used the abuse to justify my behavior.

—      —      —

During the last few years we were together I had uncovered a few suspicious items, like gas receipts, and an extra birthday card he could not account for. When confronted, he admitted that while in Reno without me he had bumped into a waitress he used to date. Later, I found this to be a fabrication on his part, a cover-up for the truth. In anger, I sailed over to the Cadillac dealership, purchased a brand-new car, and simply charged it to him. I also threw him out, but he came back with his tail between his legs a few days later, promising never again, that it was over.

When the smoke cleared after the crash, I went into the den where he had a desk and kept all his bills, paperwork, etc. He had always said, *"If anything ever happens to me, everything is in the black case in the den."* It sure was! All kinds of motel receipts and dinner tabs from Solvang and Pismo Beach area. Why I did not immediately figure out that it was our friend Linda he had been involved with, I will never know. I felt strongly that she was MY friend, and her husband was Chuck's pal.

In the mental and emotional state I was in at that time, my first reaction was to hire a private detective. I had to know who it was. He immediately indicated it was almost a sure thing it would be Linda, but I defended her and just knew she would never betray me. By Christmas day, 1979, however, I got the report from the detective, and it was definitely Linda.

—      —      —

Ego is a brutal thing and I went over the edge. In addition to all the stress of the accident, adjusting to life as a widow (which I hated), and trying to learn to handle the finances (Chuck had always done that), to find that I'd been betrayed not only by my husband, but also a by person I considered a close friend, was the straw that broke the camel's back. I had a complete breakdown, and my family and friends put me in the hospital.

The next day, full of opiates, I escaped from there and went home. Sue and my daughter Gloria, to get my mind off the whole mess, made the mistake of taking me to a movie – guess which one? Bette Midler playing Janis

Joplin in *The Rose* – drinking, taking drugs and overdosing! Looked good to me, and when we got home, I stopped by the bar in our den (which, ironically, had been stocked for the memorial service), picked up a bottle of vodka, and took a big swig. After twelve years of sobriety, it did not take much to get me smashed. My friends gathered one more time and stayed by my side the next several days. Those who knew me were honestly relieved that I took the drink. It got my attention. I did not drink the next day and have not had a drink since that night.

— — —

It took me the next two years to sort out my feelings and do what was necessary for me in order to have any peace of mind. I had to take stock, not only of Chuck, but of myself. It was a painful process; I put myself in the hospital aftercare program that I had instigated and run. Talk about humiliating. My job was still open to me, and I did go back to work for a few months, but then realized that that part of my life was also over.

I'd like to inject a few thoughts about guilt. During the last five years of my marriage, my life was better than ever. My husband was loving and attentive, and such a great companion. What I came to believe later was that it was due in part to his feelings of guilt for cheating on me. We were together more than ever, our relationship was almost perfect. Perhaps afterwards I should have thanked Linda for that period of my life? Hell, no, I'm not that sweet! I finally forgave, but removed her from my life.

What I know today is that if Chuck were alive, we would still be together. Our love and commitment to each other and our marriage were far above allowing each other's shortcomings to separate us. We had been over bumpy road before and always remained together. Perhaps our marriage was strengthened by our trials and tribulations.

Chuck had too many magnificent qualities to allow his memory to be tarnished. He was a dedicated pilot, father, and husband. A real man. In today's world, I am appalled by the multiple divorces that go on. It seems that couples now don't really try to work on things, but seem to have the attitude that the marriage is unimportant, it's not perfect, so let's split up.

Now I have exposed my "dark side," along with Chuck's, but I want you to know that they were far and away surpassed by our "bright" sides. We had a good life – lots of laughs and lots of tears, but we stayed together "'til death did us part." I loved him truly, and I know he loved me. God, how I miss that man. He used to tell me, *"Life is for the living; if anything happens to me, live it!"* I have tried to do just that, in the best way I am able.

# Part VI

# Moving On

## Moving Helped Me Move On

After the loss of my husband in 1979, I moved from Palos Verdes to Palm Springs, to Hawaii, to Florida, and back to Palos Verdes. I don't regret all the moving I've done in the last twenty-five years. The different places I lived each had their own beauty. Moving from place to place was extremely interesting, and along the way I made wonderful friends. I took to heart Chuck's view that life was for the living, so I did just that - I lived it. He also felt that a house was a building, but a home is where you live.

—     —     —

In order to survive, I got into renovating and building. This activity kept me busy and was a creative outlet for me. To buy an old house or a condominium in need of repair was a challenge that kept me going. It became addictive, but also very satisfying, to live amongst the confusion and disarray and watch things come together as I had envisioned.

I started in Palos Verdes – sold the family home, bought a condominium there, and had it re-done. Then came an old house in Palm Springs in the Las Palmas area. After that it was on to Hawaii, where I had two houses built and and another condominium fixed up. Then it was on to Destin to a new condo that I planned and decorated as it was being constructed.

When I finally returned to Palos Verdes, I purchased another older home and once again, had it torn apart and remodeled. After that I swore to knock off that activity. I'd lived in Home Depot and other paint and appliance stores for years. It was past time to settle in. You could say I'm in withdrawal, acknowledging the need to slow down a bit.

My friends and family are relieved, to say the least. I have the record for taking up more space in their address books than they had available under "G."

## Palm Springs

Palm Springs was fantastic – the mountains always changing colors as the days and weather went by. The purples, browns, grays and oranges were a sight to behold. My favorite time of the day was sunrise. It was so clear and the air so fresh. Spring, winter, and fall were good living, but when summer arrived it was "get-out-of-town time." The heat was indescribable. Shopping had to be done at sunrise or in the evening, and the only comfortable place was where there was air-conditioning.

During this period my granddaughter Shannon came to live with me. Her mother Gloria had divorced again and become addicted to prescription medicine. It got so out of control that by Shannon's 12th birthday it was necessary for her to come live with me. Gloria has since recovered and is doing quite well. This was a challenge, but with therapy and patience, we got through those years. Like it or not, the addiction disease seems to be genetic and often will occur again in a family. My family has been no exception.

—      —      —

One aspect of taking on a 12-year-old girl was that it kept me young. To watch her and her friends doing their thing was eye-opening and, at times, exhausting. Just trying to keep them in school was difficult. It got so I would not go out for groceries until late afternoon, so that I would not run into the group out for breakfast or just hanging out. At that time they were into black clothing, burgundy hair, and dead-white face makeup. It looked grotesque to me but that was "in."

I lived there for three years. Then one day in the summer, I was out by the pool, which was so hot it was like swimming in a bowl of soup. I looked around and wondered what in the world I was doing there. I tried to think where I really wanted to live. All that came to mind was the ocean in Hawaii; bobbing around in the waves, feeling as if I never wanted to go back to shore. What was I doing in the desert? I realized that I was a beach bum out of my environment. I really didn't fit in with the desert community. I didn't play tennis or golf, and was not ready to die. I contacted an old friend from high school who lived in Hawaii. She found me a place to buy on the North Shore of Oahu, and away we went.

## Hawaii

Hawaii is my favorite place on earth. It smells good, looks good, and feels good. When you see an artist's rendering of scenes of Hawaii, the colors look impossible, unless you've lived there and know the density and depth of the hues in the mountains, the flowers, and the sea. On the big island, Hawaii, the contrast of the black lava and blooming array of colors in and around it is one of my favorite sights. This spectacle can be seen on the Kona coast.

The locals I was fortunate to meet and be with taught me many lessons about life, priorities, and love. *"Go beach and talk story"* is their main philosophy and I'm all for it! They believe in nature and all its glory as their proof of God, and I have come to agree. They have a way of loving each other that is unique. If an unmarried daughter shows up pregnant, there is no shame or shock. What they do is celebrate the gift of a new human soul among them.

If you become friends with them, you are automatically a member of the family unit. I know to this day that should I return, knock on the door of one or more of those I became close to, and say I have no money and no place to live, I would be welcomed with open arms, taken in, and cared for. To them, it's no big deal. If we could all live by these simple and loving ideals, it might just be a better world.

—       —       —

Shortly after moving to Hawaii, Shannon decided to return to her mother in San Diego and get serious about school. Later, she and I visited my friend Dottie in Virginia, which led to her attending George Mason University and living at Dottie's. While there, she met and then married a guy named Jeff. It didn't last, but my friendship with him did.

—       —       —

Next in line was my grandson Leon. His mother, Patricia, was having difficulty with drugs and alcohol, and he moved in with me at age 12.

Back to therapy we went. With unconditional love, which gave him dignity and security, he did very well. He was the easiest human I have ever shared a home with. A loving, trusting soul.

When he was attending Kaneohe High School, he became friends with a local boy. Joe lived with his family out in the country. They had no luxuries as we know them, but they did have a pool table in the yard. This seemed to be important to all of them, and they loved to play the game. They also spent a lot of time at the beach. Leon was convinced that being in their home in the country was the healthiest place in the world. With all the green surrounding them, he knew there was more oxygen there.

—       —       —

When Hurricane Iniki struck the islands, the roof of their house was blown away. (I should mention it was not in great shape to begin with.) The Red Cross took them in and gave them money to replace the roof. Their answer to that was to put a huge tarp on the roof and buy a new entertainment center. I think that illustrates pretty clearly the difference in our priorities, and I tend to think that in many ways they had the right idea.

—       —       —

They adopted Leon as a "haole" son. When we left Hawaii in 1994, Joe's mother wrote the following poem for Leon, and I still cry when I read it.

*The time had come for you to leave after graduating from school.*
*You should be given a certificate and with honors, in backyard pool.*
*But put all joking and laughing on the side, and reminisce along with me.*
*I remember when Joe brought you home, your friendship was visible to see.*
*The bond between you two boys grew stronger every day.*
*The sharing and growing relationship meant a lot in every way.*
*I guess that's when I made a choice, to hanai a haole boy,*
*Because of the crazy things you both did, it was obvious your sharing was a joy.*
*Every time somebody asked me, "Who is that haole kid?"*
*I introduced you as my haole son, and I thought I saw you grin.*

*P.S.  I still have no money, but a part of my heart belongs to you.*
                    *Joe's Mom, Kaneohe, HI, 1994*

## Destin

After Hawaii came Destin, Florida.  The move this time was motivated by the fact that I was aging and knew I should be back on the mainland, closer to my children.  It was also not too far from Pensacola, and I did remember the warm gulf water and those beaches with sand like white sugar.

Destin is on the panhandle of Florida, an area known as the "Redneck Riviera."  Life was good there, but after Hawaii, the winters were too cold.  There was also a problem with hurricanes.  We had one hit us head on.  My condominium was on a narrow peninsula that ran between the harbor and the gulf.  It was a perfect location but disastrous in a hurricane.  We had to evacuate.  On returning, our area looked like Death Valley.  A twelve-foot water swell had wiped out all the garages, elevators, and first floors.  We were forced to rent until repairs could be made.

—    —    —

Around this time Leon moved back to San Diego to study electronics at trade school, and at this point I gave up and moved back to Palos Verdes, where Chuck and I had raised our children.  If I had any roots at all, it was there.  It drove my kids crazy when I kept moving around, but life is short, and I wanted to keep going and experiencing as much as possible, one day at a time.

## There's No Place Like Home

Now that I've bared my soul (at least to the extent my memory and modesty allow) about my years during childhood, the Depression, WWII, marriage, kids, alcoholism, infidelity, recovery, and survival, I think it only fitting that I tell a little about who, what, and where I am now.

As of the printing of this book, I have reached the ripe old age of eighty-six. I am still active in my recovery program. I do volunteer work at the House of Hope. The clientele at the house are of course much younger than I am, but then sometimes I feel most of the world is! We get them from jail, off the street, and from a variety of backgrounds. The girls refer to me as their "Grandma" and I cherish every moment I spend with them. They give me so much love it warms my heart and lights up my days.

I can honestly say that in the process of recovery I have never encountered such beautiful spirits as these women. They are so loving, caring, and full of gratitude that they constantly overwhelm me. It is indeed a gift and honor to do my best to try to help them. It is hard to be with them and visualize what their lives were like before coming in for treatment.

I have a secret belief that those of us caught up in the world of addiction are perhaps spiritually bankrupt while using – hoping to find serenity but losing it in the fleeting euphoria of our drug of choice.

–    –    –

Mentally, I do not feel my age. Physically, now, that's another story! At this stage of my life, if you don't get me in the morning, forget it. I tell friends and family that if they need help after 9 p.m., don't call me, dial 911. I mean it, and they know it. Little tasks get bigger, and maintenance of the body parts gets more frequent and necessary. Sort of pathetic but we have to keep adjusting to our environment and capabilities.

Another requirement I have now is reclining chairs and flushing toilets. For your general information, toilets get shorter and smaller and harder to get off of as the so-called aging process sets in.

The one subject I have personally committed myself to never ever discuss, no matter what, is "bowel movements." Yes, I am aware of how greatly important they become in our later years. I remember my sister-in-law, Grace, telling us about running into two old ladies parked on the side of the road down in Alabama. They were standing by their car near a wooded area. Grace thought perhaps they had a problem, so she pulled over to see if they needed help. When she approached them, they assured her they were just splendid, that they had both had great BMs that morning and just had to get out of the house to enjoy the day. Heaven help me if my life and feelings ever come to revolve around that body function.

—    —    —

As I've gotten older, I've really come to appreciate simple pleasures, and I resort to some strange activities in order to get a "rush." For instance, while preparing to retire for the night, doing my chores, teeth, face, etc., I toss my nightgown in the dryer on high heat. I get naked and wow, when that nightie hits my chilled body it is a real treat. It reminds me of my childhood.

The viruses that attack the hard drive in my head are scary. Yes, short-term memory is a thing of the past, but I feel pretty good about how much I've been able to recall about my earlier years. I get to feeling like an old used car, almost ready for the graveyard. I keep telling my doctors they need to open up a garage for us elders so we could check in every morning and get oiled and gassed up for the day.

—    —    —

When I reached the ripe old age of 80, I began to think I needed to live some place where I'd be taken care of if need be. My granddaughter and others tried to convince me to wait until I actually needed the extra help, but I insisted on going into a retirement community. The last thing I wanted in life was to become a burden on my children.

In the retirement community we had our individual condos, but went to the main building for breakfast and dinner. It reminded me of going to the chow hall during my time in the service, except I didn't have to scrape my plate. There were other similarities to military life. We had a dress code – informal in the morning, no slippers allowed, and for the evening meal we dressed casually, but nicely. I honestly thought this would be good for me, but in the end I found it boring and unnecessary. I just didn't fit in.

Ambulances and fire trucks came quite frequently, what with strokes and people who fell down and couldn't get up. Jokingly, I suggested they get a bulletin board with color-coded pins to keep track of which hospital our residents were in. By George, they put one up!

Some of the elderly residents were rescued totally naked, and at our age, that's not a pretty sight. My greatest fear is for those young paramedics and firemen, who may never have a normal sex life after that.

I also had the same feelings that I had during the war. I was reluctant to get to know people for fear of losing them. After seeing illness and death every day, I wanted to be back around younger folk, in the real world.

I gave up after about 6 months and moved back to Palos Verdes into a condo that I truly treasure. I feel sure now that this is my home. I have comfort, security, convenience and old friends and family near by. In the long run, like Dorothy in Kansas, there's no place like home.

# Part VII

# Searching for Peace
# Amid a World in Turmoil

## September 11th

Since the death of my husband in a plane crash on October 31, 1979, I've developed the habit of sleeping with my television on all night. It seemed to stop my nightmares of being on an airplane as it crashed into a building.

The morning of September 11, 2001, I was awakened by the sight of the first jet flying into the World Trade Center in New York City. My first reaction was, *"My God, how did that flight ever get lost or confused enough to hit that skyscraper?"* It was a clear, beautiful day in New York. I got up, went upstairs to get my coffee, turned the television on, and then the second plane hit the other tower. *"Dear God in heaven, what is happening?"* We all know that the third plane then went into the Pentagon, followed by the crash of a fourth plane in the Pennsylvania countryside.

—    —    —

I was immobilized. I became non-functional and felt like a robot, going about necessary human activities, but mentally blank. It was overwhelming – too much for my brain and emotions to even begin to deal with.

I became transfixed by the television – horrified, sad beyond belief, angry, frustrated, and withdrawn. My son was with me, and he went to work that day, as did others who had jobs to go to. How they did it is beyond my comprehension. The next few days are a blank.

One thing I remember is that I made cauliflower cheese soup. When all else fails, I go to my kitchen and cook. It seems to be the one thing I can do that doesn't require thinking.

I experienced feelings of sinking into a bottomless pit of darkness, similar to the feelings I had after the tragic crash of my husband's plane. My head got to the point that I felt it would literally blow up. My brain pushed against my skull and wanted out. Exhaustion hit and I could do absolutely nothing but sit and stare like a zombie.

Every aspect of what was happening was so daunting. Clearly, this generation would be forced to deal with a new kind of war. Terrorism had become a fact of life and the prospects were frightening, to say the least.

—    —    —

During the next several days, it felt like I was treading water, trying to stay afloat. Rumors were flying, and it seemed that no one, absolutely no one, really knew or understood what we could or should do. Some of my friends had rabid ideas. We certainly had an enemy after us with a hatred and vengeance unlike any we'd really known before.

One day when my anger was quite intense, I found myself actually trying to find someone or something I could verbally assault. It happened to be a day when I was called back for a second mammogram. Something needed to be re-checked. The office where the first exam was done informed me that I had to go to a different location for the second one. Oh, great! How dare they schedule me at a different location without informing me? I went sailing over to the hospital, determined when I got there to really let them know how I felt about their incompetence, lack of consideration, and so on.

When I arrived, the little old lady volunteer behind the desk was so sweet and gentle that she took all the anger and rage from me. It felt as if the air had been let out of my balloon. By the time I got through with the mammogram and ultra-sound, and found that all was okay, I had calmed down, and of course was relieved. To be honest, while the procedure was going on, I didn't even care about the results. At one point, I wanted to tell them to take the damn boob off if they wanted to.

—      —      —

Eventually I got to the stage where I had to realize that it was out of my control, and I had to trust in our government and my God. I am obviously too old to participate. I can only display my beloved flag and contribute my prayers and everlasting love for my country. I pray that God will lead our men who must make our decisions for us.

The heroism we were watching on the tube was magnificent. I hold true to my basic belief that the majority of Americans, regardless of ethnic background, religious beliefs, age, or sex, are selfless and brave in times of crisis. Once again they rose to heights of bravery which were dazzling to behold.

My heart is bleeding for the thousands of lost souls and their beloved families and friends. I am concerned for the children who are coming of age in this dark time for our country, with the fear, anger, mistrust, and frustration that comes with it. I also have pity and compassion for the mothers and fathers with military-age children. When our country calls, it will be their brave sons and daughters who will risk life and limb responding to this vague but very real threat.

—      —      —

I began to sort out some of my feelings and thoughts, and could not help but compare it all to the experience of World War II. Yes, those lost at Pearl Harbor were military and it was the start of that war, but the young boys and civilians lost were human beings with families and loved ones. My mourning includes other wars and tragedies we have endured, including

Korea, Vietnam, Oklahoma City, and other events that have torn us apart.

I've also continued to have a problem with what we did at Hiroshima and Nagasaki. More than two hundred thousand civilians were killed. Maybe it was a necessary step, taken to end the war, but I've never been able to make peace within myself regarding this act by our country. I'm well aware that it's in the past and nothing can be done to change it, but it makes me sad. I'm not even sure why my mind keeps going to the subject, but it does. Right or wrong, we did it, and we cannot undo it.

—　　　—　　　—

Ugly rumors reached me regarding the attacks of Sept. 11th. For example, that it was "set up" to sway the country in favor of Bush. Or that the implosion of the two towers in New York wasn't possible from the impact of the airplanes. Some as repugnant and ridiculous as there having been no Jews in the towers when they fell. And on and on. While there is plenty about the Bush administration that I revile and which makes me mistrust them, I personally cannot afford to play around with too much of this talk. It is too devastating to contemplate.

Once again, it seems to have taken a war to unite us, although I am afraid the unity we felt right after the attacks has dissolved into a gigantic divide because of the disastrous decision to attack Iraq. Similarly, the goodwill shown towards this country after Sept. 11th has been squandered by our heavy-handed and misguided response to it. No one seems to agree on how best to fight this new war, and we are losing friends with every passing day.

We have bigots and the ignorant among us, who would tar all Muslims with the acts of a few. There must be some way to make them understand that we cannot condemn whole groups or nations for the minority who are evil. God, when will we realize we are all human, and live and let live? Not in my lifetime, I'm afraid. Once again I'm reminded of my lack of control and/or power, and must let go. I suppose I'll leave this planet never understanding man's inhumanity to man. It still is, and always has been, a mystery to me. We are given the freedom of choice, but some of us don't seem able to exercise it except at the expense of others.

The terrorists succeeded in many ways by instilling fear and apprehension in us. I see it in my friends and family, and sweeping over the whole country. The rumors fly and we are powerless. I can only exert control over my life, and do the best I can on a daily basis to be kind and loving to those I come in contact with, including family, friends, and salespeople. Even while driving in the car, politeness and consideration do pay off. I get back what

On a cruise to Alaska to celebrate the 50th Anniversary of our graduation from Collingswood High School. L to R: Rita, Helen, Jayne, Mary and Eva.

The house I renovated on Sunset Beach, on the North Shore of Oahu, Hawaii.

I give and it feels good. Life goes on, the good along with the bad, and I'm grateful for today.

## Family and Friends Are What It's All About

One of the things I've learned along the way is that my inner peace and happiness depends on my attitude. Love of family and friends is what really counts. Among my many blessings are four children, two grandchildren, and two great-grandchildren. As of the printing of this book, here's what they're up to:

Charlene, my oldest daughter (the one I call my "flower child"), changed her name to Alanah and lives in Santa Barbara. Her outlook on life is amazing. She has really worked hard seeking spirituality and self-knowledge.

Gloria, my middle daughter, is living a quiet, stress-free life in San Diego.

Patricia, my youngest daughter, ended up in South Carolina. She is happily married and seems content to be a "Southerner."

Charles, my only son, is a miracle. We are closer than ever after many years, during which I traveled much and he established himself. He drives his own car, has a good job, and lives in Whittier, about a half hour from me.

Shannon, my only granddaughter, and her husband Rene live in San Diego, and have two children, Harrison and Rhiannon.

Leon, my only grandson, is in San Diego, working in electronics.

Harrison and Rhiannon, my great-grandchildren are a joy to me and I feel so lucky to have lived long enough to know them. They call me GG for great-grandmother. What a gift they are. At least, if they don't kill me! One day with them, and I'm ready for a week's rest. Such energy, and being the idiot that I am, I still try to keep up with them. When I go to visit them, I say I'm going down to let the kids abuse me.

## Simple Pleasures

I've come to realize I need space around me and windows to the outside world. I want to feel a part of it, not isolated from it. We learn and grow as we live. The only control I have seems to be over my television remote control, if the battery is working. I know that the biggest problem I have in life is the one I see when I look in a mirror.

My son Charlie as a child, and all grown up.

My daughter Alanah with my great-granddaughter Rhiannon.

My daughter Gloria with Harrison.

My granddaughter Shannon, her husband Rene, & Harrison.

My great-grandchildren Harrison & Rhiannon.

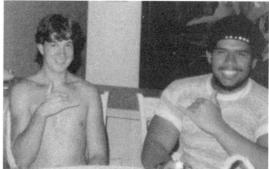

My daughter Patricia with my grandson Leon, and Leon with his friend Joe in Hawaii.

The beach and the ocean are my favorite places for getting in touch with my spirituality and myself. They soothe my body and soul, and renew my spirit. When I enter the water and go out past the breakers to swim or float, I can feel the the stress and turmoil of daily living just melt away. The sounds, smells and feelings I experience are sheer delight. I become a grain of sand, a part of the universe, and who and what I am become clear to me.

When I stretch out on the warm sand, I can hear the roar of the waves crashing on the shore. I enjoy watching the sea gulls swooping down to the sea, searching for food, calling to each other. They strut along the beach, hoping for a hand-out. Pelicans fly by, usually in formation, reminding me of a squadron of sea-planes on their way to an unknown destination. Children squeal with joy as they play and discover a whole new world. The salty breezes caress my body. The warm sun toasts me. I am as close to nirvana as I think it is possible to be.

If there is more than one life and I've been here before, I must have been one of those sand crabs that run in and out of the water at the shoreline. To be honest, when I return from the beach, I hate to shower off the sand and salt, it feels so good. You could call me a real beach bum.

–     –     –

I'm truly grateful for all aspects my life – pain and sorrow, joy and happiness. Without the pain, I wouldn't have known joy. It has been an interesting and rewarding journey.

I've learned that there are no big deals. Whatever happens, I try to remember that in a week, a month, or a year, it will not be of great importance in the overall picture of my life. Stand still and let it hurt. It will pass and it will change.

Anger and resentment will only hurt me. I would rather trust and love than be suspicious and hate. This keeps me at peace within.

When I accept the humanity in my fellow man, they accept my humanity. To be human is not to strive to be perfect - it is to progress and improve. Forgiveness and acceptance are the keys to freedom. Go with the flow. Things are as they are supposed to be. I have what I refer to as "green lights" that guide me. When I hit roadblocks, I try to change direction and stay flexible. At all times, I trust in my concept of a Higher Power. It works.

–     –     –

Aloha and sweet dreams. I hear the Fat Lady singing. She gets louder all the time.

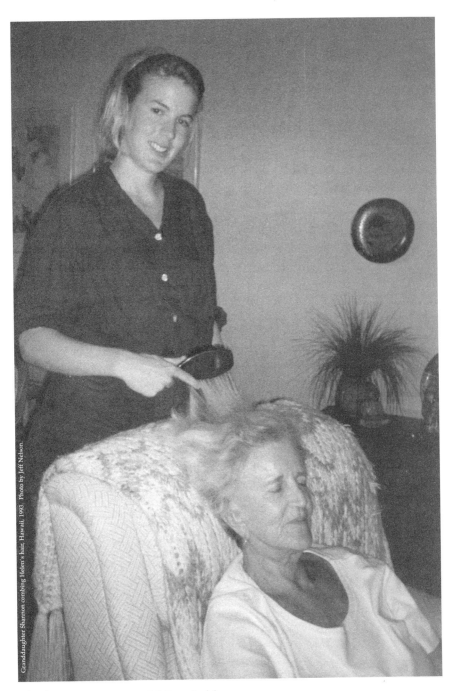

Granddaughter Shannon combing Helen's hair, Hawaii, 1993. Photo by Jeff Nelson.

Ah, the contentment and bliss of old age...